CARVING
IN THE ROUND

CARVING
IN THE ROUND

7 Projects to Take Your First Steps in the Art

ANDREW THOMAS

The Taunton Press

For Christine x

The Taunton Press, Inc., 63 South Main Street
P.O. Box 5506, Newtown, CT 06470-5506
e-mail: tp@taunton.com

First published 2012 by
Guild of Master Craftsman Publications Ltd
Castle Place, 166 High Street, Lewes,
East Sussex BN7 1XU

Library of Congress Cataloging-in-Publication Data in progress
ISBN 978 1 62113 008 6

Publisher Jonathan Bailey
Production Manager Jim Bulley
Managing Editor Gerrie Purcell
Senior Project Editor Dominique Page
Editor Simon Smith
Managing Art Editor Gilda Pacitti
Designer Chloë Alexander

Set in DIN
Color origination by GMC Reprographics
Printed and bound by Hung Hing Offset

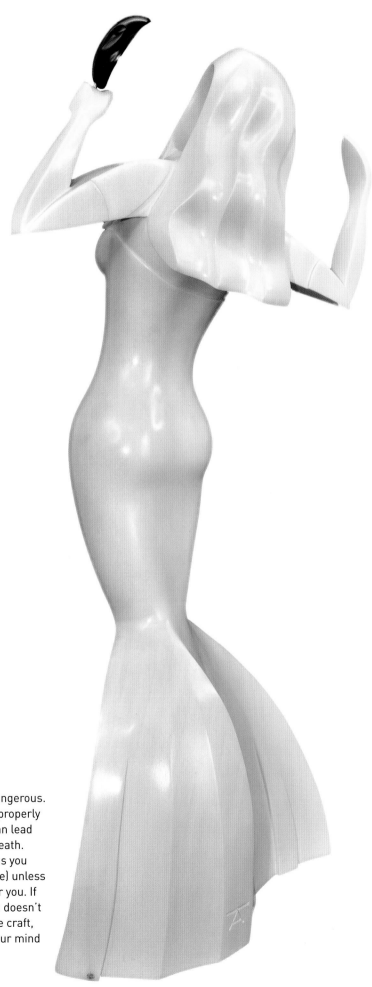

About Your Safety

Working wood is inherently dangerous.
Using hand or power tools improperly
or ignoring safety practices can lead
to permanent injury or even death.
Don't try to perform operations you
learn about here (or elsewhere) unless
you're certain they are safe for you. If
something about an operation doesn't
feel right, don't do it. Enjoy the craft,
but keep safety foremost in your mind
whenever you're in the shop.

Contents

PART TWO **THE PROJECTS**

Introduction

THE ART OF CREATING THREE-DIMENSIONAL FORMS IN WOOD – WHETHER INTRICATE CARVINGS OF A TRADITIONAL NATURE, OR ELEGANT CONTEMPORARY FORMS SUCH AS THOSE BY THE GREATS HENRY MOORE AND BARBARA HEPWORTH – IS AN EXTREMELY REWARDING AND PLEASURABLE EXPERIENCE THAT ANYONE CAN EMBRACE AND LEARN.

This book is designed to give you a taste both of contemporary and traditional styles, taking you on a journey from a very simple but elegant abstract form through to the complex realistic study of a humpback whale – two very different disciplines, both equally important.

Success in creating a piece of three-dimensional art comes from mastering and balancing two main disciplines: the effective manipulation of the material and comprehending the complexities of designing a balanced form in three dimensions. Both are of equal value and dependent on each other for success; therefore an even balance should be struck between them for the progressive advancement of the learner. One of the unfortunate misunderstandings of this subject is to put too much emphasis on the technical area of development without the important balance of creativity. This inevitably results in the learner experiencing the frustration of not being able to design their own projects on which to apply the techniques that they have learned and, ultimately, being faced with the uninspiring option of copying the work of other people.

There are various different philosophies and approaches to teaching woodcarving. The method I have structured enables you to develop your skills quickly, effectively and enjoyably. This encourages and teaches you to choose a diversity of subjects and to employ an array of styles, so that you are consistently learning different techniques, problem solving new issues and using your inner creativity to develop your imagination and designing skills. In practice, this approach to learning divides the subject into two areas: realistic technical projects (realism) and freedom-of-expression forms (abstract). The realistic technical projects require an in-depth study of the anatomy and form of real-life subjects and the use of various methods of measuring, tool techniques and observation to replicate the subject as accurately as possible. These studies and techniques are of the utmost importance in order to master the medium; although, in practice, they are quite intense as there is little leeway for artistic freedom.

The freedom-of-expression forms are a refreshing balance to the realistic studies, as they require us to engage our inner creativity in conjunction with the elements and principles of design. They demand imagination to develop a form in relation to a concept or message you wish to express. The process of creating the sculpture is also different, as you must sensitively feel your way into the form, which will give you a vital understanding of balance and harmony and will naturally develop your intuition and perception of three-dimensional work. This much freer application of creativity is extremely rewarding and pleasurable.

If you embrace these two distinct branches of three-dimensional work, then over time you will become capable of uniting them to supreme effect, creating original forms in whatever style or technique you wish to employ.

This book has been created with the same ethos, to give you a structured, methodical and effective introduction to working in three dimensions with the beautiful, tactile medium of wood. Each of the projects has been carefully chosen and designed to build progressively on your technical and creative skills from one project to the next. Each can be either copied to the letter or adapted to your own design. Ultimately, the aim is to help you develop these important skills effectively – but equally to enjoy the experience and feel inspired to continue your creative journey.

The book can be used in two ways. If you are a beginner, then I would strongly encourage you to utilize it as a course, working your way through each of the projects in the order they appear in the book. This will teach you the fundamental disciplines of the subject, build your confidence and knowledge and give you a fabulous foundation from which to advance. If you are a beginner, then I would also recommend that you consider designing and making your own projects in between the ones provided, as this will underpin the techniques you have learned and help independent development. If, however, you are at an intermediate or advanced level, then you can simply choose which piece you believe would benefit you, as they are all complete, standalone projects.

Whatever your level of ability, I would advise that you always read through the entire project before you begin, and examine the stage pictures and finished images (A, B, C, etc.) to give you a

'Violin' by Andrew Thomas.

clear understanding of what you are trying to achieve and a visual reference of how the project develops.

GOLDEN RULES Always try to be innovative and experimental. Push yourself when it comes to designing and bringing your own ideas and concepts to life. Most importantly, keep the design simple but ensure that all of the elements remain in harmony. Along with diversity of subject and style, these will be the keys to your progression and development as an independent artist. If you can design your own forms, then you will never be lost for ideas.

THE BASICS

Woodcarving, by its very nature, has many fundamental areas of technical information that one must learn in order to effectively and enjoyably achieve a good result. The following chapters outline the initial information that you will need to get you started and are a foundation upon which you can build your knowledge and experience.

At the end of Part One you will find a simple exercise to help you understand grain direction. This is designed as an introduction to woodcarving for the beginner and offers valuable practical experience working with the carving tools and the medium, which will be of great benefit to complete before you start work on the projects.

TOOLS

THERE IS A WIDE RANGE OF WOODCARVING TOOLS AVAILABLE TODAY, FROM SMALL PALM GOUGES TO FLEXIBLE-BLADE GOUGES, MICROCARVING TOOLS TO SCORPS. THEY COME IN ALL SHAPES AND SIZES AND FROM MANY DIFFERENT MANUFACTURERS. THIS LEVEL OF CHOICE CAN BE VERY CONFUSING FOR THE BEGINNER, AND CARE IS NEEDED SO THAT MONEY IS NOT INVESTED IN THE WRONG CHOICE OF TOOLS.

This chapter has been kept as concise as possible so as not to overwhelm the beginner but instead to provide the essential information. It introduces the chisel and gouge numbering systems, the types of tools that are available, explains what to be aware of when purchasing tools and what to avoid, ultimately so that you can make informed choices in the future.

Chisels and gouges

All of the chisels and gouges that are used for woodcarving are numbered according to the curvature of their cutting edge, which is called the sweep. Just to confuse things, there are two numbering systems that are generally in use: the Sheffield and the Swiss. Throughout this book, the Swiss system is quoted. However, for cross reference you will find an overview of both numbering systems on pages 22–25.

COMPARING THE SHEFFIELD AND SWISS NUMBERING SYSTEMS

If you try to find a formula that explains the differences between the Sheffield and Swiss numbering systems, you could find yourself somewhat confused, as there seems to be quite a lot of conflicting information on the subject. This is understandable, because the Swiss have in fact added two new sweeps in recent years: No. 4 and No. 6. To untangle some of the confusion between the systems, we can start by clarifying the exact differences to date. Unfortunately, this is still not a straightforward process of listing equivalent numbers, as some of the Swiss sweeps fall in between the Sheffield ones. The table below shows a comparison of the Sheffield and Swiss tool sizes.

Sheffield	Swiss
No. 1	No. 1
No. 2	No. 1S
No. 3	No. 2
No. 4	No. 3 – almost identical to Sheffield No. 4
	No. 4 – halfway between the Sheffield No. 4 and No. 5
No. 5	No. 5 – almost identical to Sheffield
No. 6	No. 6 – fractionally less curved than the Sheffield No. 6
No. 7	No. 7 – halfway between the Sheffield No. 6 and No. 7
No. 8	No. 8 – fractionally less curved than the Sheffield No. 8
No. 9	No. 9
No. 10	There is no equivalent to the Sheffield No. 10 in the Swiss range to date
No. 11	No. 11 – far more acute ellipse around its cutting edge than the Sheffield No. 11
No. 39	No. 12

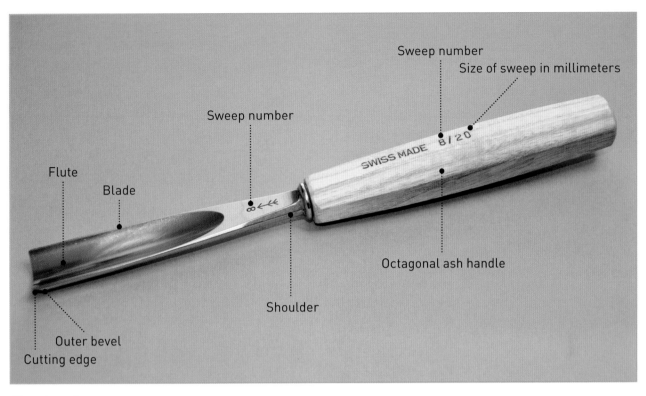

Sweep number

Size of sweep in millimeters

Sweep number

Flute

Blade

SWISS MADE 8/20

Octagonal ash handle

Shoulder

Outer bevel
Cutting edge

The anatomy of a gouge.

Most tools have the sweep number (the curve of the cutting edge) stamped on the metal shank of the blade, and some also have it on the handles alongside the size of the sweep in millimeters. See the example pictured above: the '8' on the metal shank refers to the sweep number, and the '8/20' stamped on the handle means that the tool is 20mm (¾in.) wide with a No. 8 sweep. It is

advisable to learn the theory of the numbering system as soon as you start to carve, as doing so will help you to think in terms of a contour's curvature and what sweep you will need to use to produce it.

This book mainly features the most commonly used numbers, which range from No. 1 to No. 12 and are quite logical in their numerical order.

Starting with No. 1 then, this is a straight, flat tool, which we call a chisel. If No. 1/12mm is referred to in the text, it means a flat chisel that is 12mm (½in.) wide. No. 1 chisels are limited in their use because of the straight cutting edge, although they are particularly useful for letter cutting. There is also a No. 1S (S = Skew), which is essentially the same tool as the No. 1, but with the cutting edge ground to an angle of 45 degrees. It is a very useful tool for a number of applications, especially working into angled areas – such as the corners of eyes or mouths – to chip out the waste that a square-edged tool cannot reach.

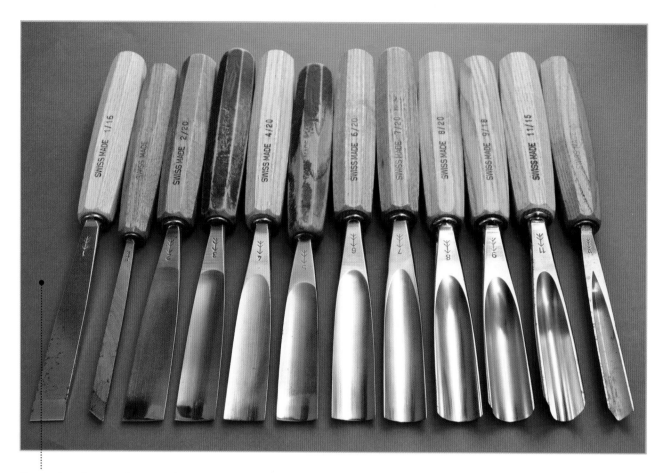

Study the picture above and examine the sweep numbers from left to right from 1 to 12. Note the gradual increase of the curvature of the cutting edges as the numbers increase. Remember, there is no No. 10 in the Swiss numbering system. No. 2 is the first sweep in the range of gouges, which has the least acute curvature on the cutting edge (see third from the left).

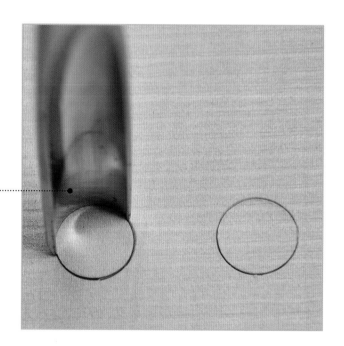

After No. 2 each subsequent sweep becomes more acutely curved until we reach No. 9, which is a perfect semicircle (as seen in the picture on the right). All of the sweep numbers from 2 to 9 are an arc of a circle and all have multiple uses for all forms of shaping, including detailing, hollowing, texturing, relieving, convexing and channeling.

The No. 11 – also known as a veiner or fluter because of the deep channel that it creates – is a U-shaped gouge that is used for many jobs but is particularly effective for producing hair and fabric folds. Several different sizes are usually used in combination with each other to create the crease or channel and realistically form the complicated contours of the original subject.

The No. 12 is a V-Tool, so called from its shape. This has a 60-degree angle and is the most useful all-rounder, but other V-Tools are the No. 13 (90 degrees), No. 14 (55 degrees), No. 15 (45 degrees) and No. 16 (35 degrees). V-Tools have a multitude of applications, including, to mention just a few, detailing, sketching lines around details, producing deep grooves to help separate different depths and sharpening and straightening the inner edges of angled corners.

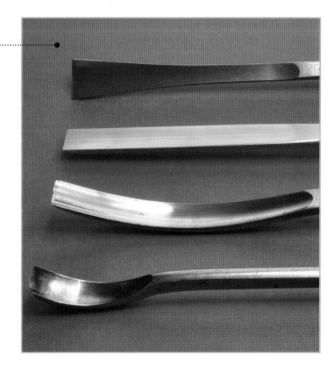

All carving tools are available in a wide range of sizes from 1–40mm but do vary a little in width depending on the sweep number. They also come in quite a few different styles of blade shape, some of which are more limited in their size ranges. Several of these variations are shown here, including (from front to back) the spoon, or short-front bent, long, or salmon bend, straight and fishtail. You can also get, among others, the reverse, or back-bent, dog leg, macaroni, fluteroni and backeroni. Most of these are used for very specialized work undertaken by church restorers and other professional artisans and craftspeople. But for the purposes of this book we shall only be using straight ones for the projects and will therefore focus on these.

This is just a small selection of the many knives that are available for carving. The Schaller knife on the left (made by Pfeil) is the best option for a beginner to learn with.

Knives

The woodcarver's knife is an exceptionally versatile, useful tool and is an essential addition to your toolkit. Knives are available in various shapes and sizes: some are made for specific applications but many are of little use for the beginner, so you need to know what you're looking for before making a purchase.

The technique of using the knife with directional control is likened to drawing with a pencil, so for optimum balance and control, the nearer your fingers are to the cutting tip of the blade, the easier it will be to direct it accurately. Thus, woodcarving knives with the shortest blades are a far better option for the beginner than the longer ones. The Schaller knife (see far left in the picture above) has a rounded back edge when compared with the flat back edges of the other knives, which facilitates even better directional control and is a good choice for any woodcarver, especially the beginner.

Buying woodcarving tools

There are many brands of tools available, and they vary considerably in quality and price. In my opinion, some of the better ones include Pfeil (Swiss system), Stubai (Sheffield system), Kirschen (Sheffield system) and Henry Taylor (Sheffield system). Ultimately, you get what you pay for, and the best advice would be to pay that little bit extra for good-quality tools that are nicely balanced, comfortable to use and will last a lifetime, rather than working around the shortcomings of cheaper options.

A good-quality tool is comprised of the following elements:

1 The overall quality of construction, including the balance and the handle

2 How thin the steel blade is

3 How long the blade keeps a keen edge

4 How strong the blade is

The quality of construction can be determined by how well the blades have been forged, whether the shoulders are even on both sides of the blade, how well balanced the tool feels when working with it and how well the handle has been fitted to the blade.

Each manufacturer has its own unique form of steel composite that is used for its blades. The composite is often a well-guarded secret, but the better ones advertise a high carbon or special alloy steel content, tempered (heat treated) to HRC 59–61 (HRC is the Rockwell Hardness scale, a method of measuring the hardness of material and its resistance to penetration), making them very thin but extremely strong with excellent edge-holding properties. They will also come honed and ready to use, which is a real advantage for the beginner.

Seven different manufactures of gouges, from left to right: Stubai, Pfeil, Kirschen, Marples (old), Henry Taylor, Tiranti and Ashley Isles.

HANDLES

The handles of the tools are generally available in two different styles: either rounded/elliptical or hexagonal. The rounded ones are perhaps slightly more comfortable in the palm of the hand, especially at the point of pressure. However, due to their curved shape, they must be placed very carefully on the bench as they can easily roll into each other, potentially damaging the cutting edge or, even worse, roll off the bench in the direction of your legs and feet! The hexagonal-shaped handles, on the other hand, do not roll as easily and have a very good grip. The only disadvantage to them is that after working for some time they can feel rather sharp in the palm at the point of pressure. The simple remedy for this problem is to round over the back edge slightly with a piece of 100-grit sandpaper to soften the angled edges at this end.

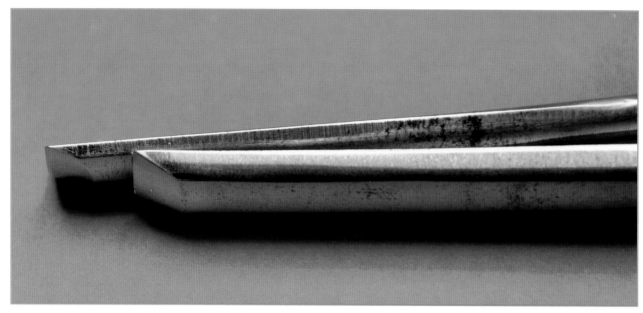

These two gouges are identical in sweep and size, but the lower blade is almost twice as thick as the one above it because of the different steel composites used in its manufacture. This will not feel as well balanced or pleasurable to use as the thinner one, making it the less desirable option.

PURCHASING SECONDHAND

Buying secondhand woodcarving tools is something of a lottery and not really recommended to any beginner woodcarver for several reasons. First, it is always possible that the previous owner may have overheated the edge of the blade when grinding the tool, which may not be obvious just from looking at it. If this is the case, the tool will not keep its edge for very long and will be brittle and prone to breaking, and to cure this would require that the blade be re-tempered. Second, the blade might be considerably shorter than a new one, as it may have been worn away over a long period of time and usage. Finally, secondhand tools are generally not particularly cheap to buy so don't really offer good value for money, unlike a brand-new, razor-sharp, quality tool that will last you a lifetime.

CARVING SETS

Most manufacturers of woodcarving tools offer sets of chisels and gouges, which might seem to be a cost-effective way of purchasing your first tools. What isn't so obvious to the beginner is that you will probably have several tools in the set that you will more than likely never use. It is far better practice to build up your tool selection slowly, one or two at a time as and when you need them, specifically for the different projects and subjects that you are working on. When you become more experienced and have a better understanding of the subject, you will naturally be interested in particular areas that you will want to explore further. You can then direct your tool purchases exactly to what you need, which is a logical and prudent approach to building your collection.

GOLDEN RULE When purchasing your first tools, experiment by testing one from a few different makers to see how each one differs. See how the balance feels working with them and which one feels more natural to your anatomy. If you find one or two that are very comfortable to use with good directional maneuverability, then try another one from that maker and build your collection from there. You really can't go wrong with Stubai, Pfeil, Kirschen and Henry Taylor for all-round excellence and quality, so any of those would be a very good starting point.

Building your tool collection

The projects in this book will help you to build your tool collection in a logical way, as the expense can be spread across the projects. The first of these, the Grain Direction exercise, requires just two tools; project 1, a further two; project 2, a further two; and so on. When you eventually work your way through the book to the last project, you will only need to buy two final new ones. If I were to offer general advice on the first tools you should buy, then I would suggest the following (in two batches, batch 1 being the basic essentials), which between them represent a good all-round selection:

Batch 1	Batch 2
Knife	No. 1S/5mm
No. 2/5mm	No. 2/20mm
No. 2/12mm	No. 3/30mm
No. 3/20mm	No. 8/4mm
No. 5/8mm	No. 9/7mm
No. 5/20mm	No. 12/3mm
No. 7/6mm	
No. 7/14mm	
No. 8/18mm	
No. 9/10mm	
No. 11/4mm	
No. 12/10mm	

Mallets

Mallets come in many different shapes, sizes and materials, including nylon, wood, malleable iron and brass. Most woodcarvers use wooden ones, made from either lignum vitae or beech, which are medium in weight and are unlikely to cause any damage to the handles of the chisels and gouges. Personally, I don't find these mallets very well balanced for my anatomy, nor do I find the delivery of power positive enough for particularly light or heavy work. I like to use a 1½lb (680g) malleable-iron dummy mallet, which is extremely well balanced with a firm and precise delivery of power, be it a delicate tap or a

On the left is a malleable-iron dummy mallet and on the right a lignum vitae wooden mallet.

full-on clout. I have been using the same mallet for well over 20 years now and have only damaged one handle in this time – and that was because the grain of the handle had a knot on the edge!

Which mallet suits best will vary from user to user depending on the size of your hands, wrists and arms. The best advice would be to test out several before you decide whether the weight and geometry of a particular manufacture suit and you make a purchase. Simply hold it in your hand, go through the motions of use and consider these questions:

- Does the handle fit comfortably in your hand?

- Does the center of gravity feel balanced, or does it pull on your wrist, arm or elbow?

- Is there enough weight to deliver a positive blow?

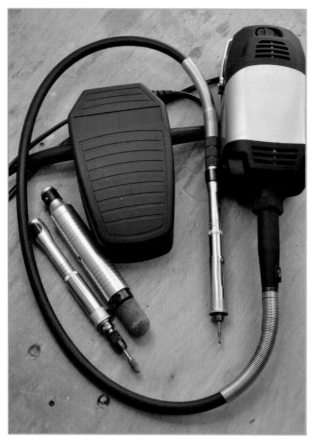

The flexible-shaft power carving unit with a variable-speed foot pedal and both heavy-duty and fine-detail handpieces. A very versatile tool for the serious carver.

Power carving

Power carving techniques will not be used for any of the projects in this book, but it is appropriate to introduce the tool, as it is an extremely valuable asset to any serious woodcarver. Power carving has become increasingly popular in recent decades, especially with bird carvers. There are two different types of units available – either a hand-held unit or a flexible-shaft machine with variable-speed foot control – both of which use various cutters for different jobs.

HAND-HELD UNIT

This is certainly the cheaper option and is useful for a variety of applications, especially stock removal, hollowing and working awkward areas of grain direction. However, because the motor is integral in the handpiece, it is quite bulky to hold and feels somewhat imbalanced. It also seems to produce a gyroscopic feeling of pressure when in use, which is certainly not ideal for creating fine detail.

FLEXIBLE-SHAFT MACHINE

Flexible-shaft machines are more expensive than hand-held units but they offer far better value for money overall, as they are extremely versatile, adaptable, simple to operate, powerful and can be used with delicate finesse on fine detail. The motor is suspended on an arm that has a rubber shaft attached to the base of the unit. Inside the rubber shaft is a flexible metal shaft that is directly attached to the motor and which transfers the power to the handpiece. The handpiece holds the cutters, or burrs, and attaches to the shaft by a simple push-click fitting, which is very quick to change. You can get a range of different handpieces for specific applications, but initially you will only need one for fine detail and a large, heavy-duty one for aggressive stock removal. The unit has a variable-speed foot pedal, which is important for use on various different applications and burrs. The variety of different cutters ranges from large carbide burrs for stock removal to small diamond burrs, which are used for smoothing or very gentle cutting. There are literally hundreds of different cutters to chose from that can be used for countless applications.

Flexible-shaft machines are extremely useful and are a must-have for any serious carver, as they are brilliant for a multitude of applications, especially deep hollowing and shaping awkward areas of grain pattern. However, learning to use one is a very different discipline from learning traditional methods and they should be used in conjunction with, and in addition to, your hand tool skills and techniques – and definitely not as a replacement. If you have a good grounding in both of these disciplines, then you will eventually be able to manipulate the medium efficiently and effectively into any shape that you wish.

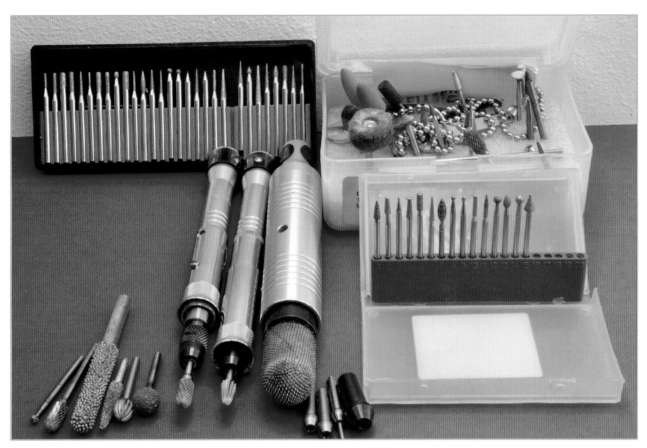

A selection of different-sized and shaped cutters for the power carving units, including carbide, diamond and high-speed steel burrs.

Without any hesitation I would advise that you purchase your hand tools first, as there will be enough initial expense with the outlay on this equipment and plenty of fundamentals and techniques for you to learn and practice from day one. When you have your workshop set up and you are more experienced with the fundamentals of woodcarving, utilizing the traditional methods and hand tools, it would then be an appropriate time to invest in a powered unit and to start gaining experience by learning the various techniques involved, if that is what you wish to do.

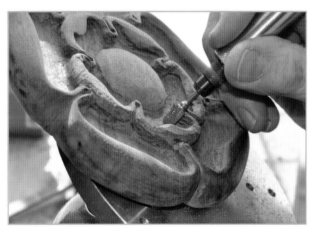

A small 'cylinder'-shaped carbide cutter is being used to hollow out the petals of a Tudor rose in American black walnut.

Carving tool shapes and profiles according to the Sheffield list

Number

Profile of cutting edge

Straight tools	Curved or Long-bent tools	Spoon or Short-bent tools	Back-bent tools	2 1/16	3 1/8	5 3/16	6 1/4	8 5/16	10 3/8	11 7/16	13 1/2	14 9/16	16 5/8	20 3/4	22 7/8
1	–	21	–												
2	–	22 23	–												
3	12	24	33												
4	13	25	34												
5	14	26	35												
6	15	27	36												
7	16	28	37												
8	17	29	38												
9	18	30	–												
10	19	31	–												
11	20	32	–												
39	40	43	–												
41	42	44	–												
45	46	–	–												

The Sheffield numbering system, as discussed on page 12, showing the curvature or shape of the sweeps (cutting edges) from No. 1 to No. 46.

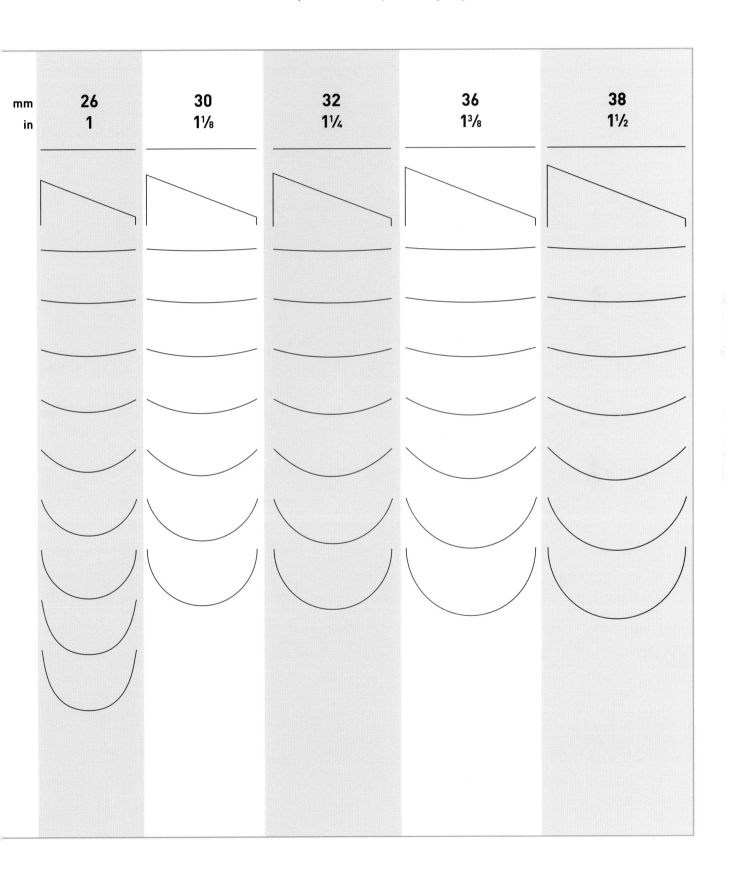

mm	**26**	**30**	**32**	**36**	**38**
in	**1**	**1⅛**	**1¼**	**1⅜**	**1½**

Carving tool shapes and profiles according to the Swiss list

1

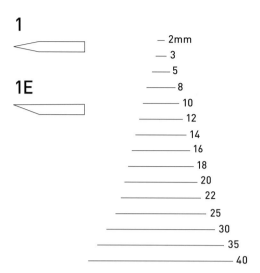

1E

1S

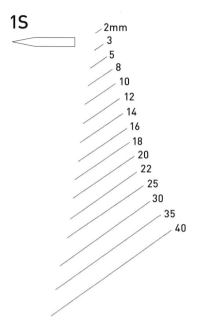

2

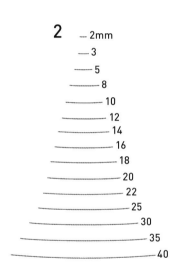

3

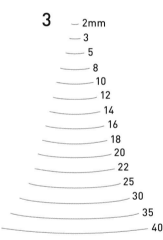

4

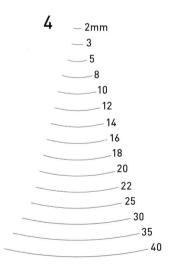

5

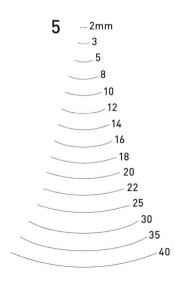

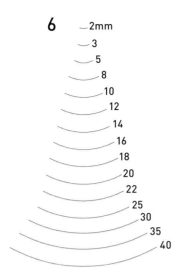

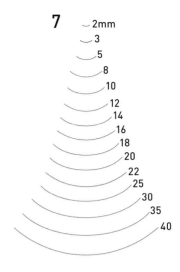

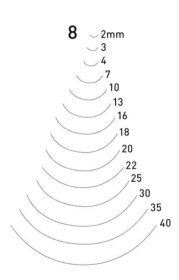

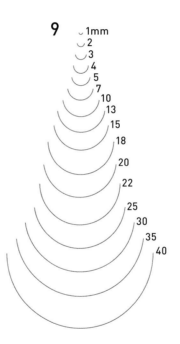

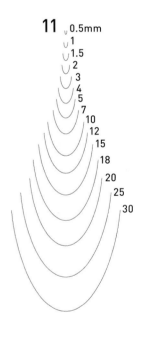

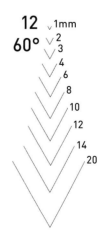

The Swiss numbering system, as discussed on page 12, showing the curvature or shape of the sweeps (cutting edges) from No. 1 to No. 12.

EQUIPMENT

SETTING UP A WORKSHOP OR STUDIO CAN BE A SUBSTANTIAL INVESTMENT FOR THE BEGINNER, SO MY ADVICE IS TO FOCUS ON THE ESSENTIALS THAT WILL ENABLE YOU TO GET STARTED, THEN EXPAND ON THE OTHER EQUIPMENT WHEN YOUR BUDGET ALLOWS. THE ESSENTIALS THAT YOU WILL NEED TO SET UP YOUR WORKSHOP ENVIRONMENT ARE THE FOLLOWING: STURDY WORKBENCH; WOODCARVING VISE (WORK POSITIONER); GOOD LIGHTING; AND AIR FILTRATION.

Safety first

It is important to watch your posture when woodcarving, as it is very easy to be focused on your project and not think about how you are positioning your neck and back while working. To help you maintain a good working posture, you should always stand when carving so that you can use the full force of your strength, from your legs up through your body to your arms, to deliver the pressure that you need to work the wood. Unless there are any health reasons to stop you, this should be taken as a firm rule to be adopted from day one.

My workbench, incorporating the height of the vise, or work positioner, is adapted for my height, so that I have an effective working posture that is also comfortable for my neck and back. I am right handed, so my right leg is back behind my body, enabling me to put the full force of my body strength behind my gouge and into my carving.

The correct combined working height of your bench and vise should be at the height of your elbow.

A sturdy workbench with a daylight magnifying lamp, a hydra clamp vise and ample surface space to place tools. The shelf underneath has large, heavy bags of clay placed on it to give it extra weight and rigidity.

Workbench

The exact dimensions of your workbench should be carefully calculated before you attempt to construct or purchase one, as it needs to be tailor-made to suit your height. This is crucial for your effective working posture and comfort. The rule of thumb is that the faceplate of your vise, in its upright position, should be at the exact height of your elbow – so you'll need to either buy, or at least know the dimensions of, your positioner before you design the size of your bench.

The workbench must be sturdy enough to be able to withstand heavy blows from the mallet and thrusts from your body power without shifting around the room as you work. It should, therefore, be quite large and rigid in its construction and built with heavy-duty materials. Recommended specifications are as follows:

Overall size (depending on your height):
Approximately 2 x 3ft (600 x 900mm)
Leg width: 4 x 4in (100 x 100mm)
Rails: 5 x 2in (125 x 50mm), jointed into the legs
Top: 2 x 6in (50 x 150mm) planks across the top
Top surface: 1in (25mm) plywood
Shelf: 1in (25mm) plywood

TIP It is a good idea to fit a shelf on the bench, as it can be loaded up with heavy materials or tools to add weight and rigidity, which helps the bench stand firm under heavy work pressure.

The hydraulically operated, quick-release, ball-and-socket vise is by far the best option for holding and positioning work.

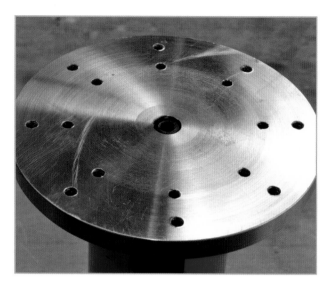

The faceplate has screw holes drilled around its surface that are used for securing the carving firmly to the vise.

Woodcarving vise

The primary functions of the woodcarving vise are twofold: to secure your work safely, thereby leaving both of your hands free to hold your tools, and to position your project at a comfortable and appropriate angle for you to work efficiently on it. Your vise is arguably the most important piece of equipment to enable you to do this. It should be strong, versatile, easy and quick to adjust and invisible to your attention, leaving you 100 per cent focused on your work.

There are a variety of vises available, but the ones that are best suited to carving are vises with a quick-release, ball-and-socket construction, which tilts 90 degrees and swivels 360 degrees, giving you full access all around your work from a single working position. These can be either mechanical devices or hydraulically operated, the latter being by far the more expensive, but ultimately one that is excellent in all regards and will last a lifetime – and probably a lot longer.

All vises will have a custom-made faceplate that attaches to their body with a number of holes in it through which you secure your carving. There are also many other methods that you can use to secure your work to your bench, including clamps, carver's screws and vises. But these are not the best or most practical options and can be very frustrating and uncomfortable to use, requiring the carver to stop regularly to make adjustments to the piece and/or their working position.

Safety first

Always secure your work to a vise, leaving both hands free to hold your tools. Never take risks trying to carve anything hand-held unless it is absolutely necessary (for more on this, see pages 50–51).

The correct positioning and type of lighting in your working environment is an essential consideration when setting up your workshop or studio.

Lighting

Appropriate lighting and how it is positioned are major considerations when setting up your workspace. Whether you are producing intricate details – such as hair, folds or facial features – or creating a gentle surface contour on an abstract sculpture, it is vital to have the correct type of correlated color temperature (CCT) light under which to work, and to help highlight any detail that might need to be adjusted.

The typical shade or CCT (measured in degrees kelvin, or K) of incandescent lighting (a warm, yellowish color) that we use in and around our homes is 2,700K. But, for workshop or studio lighting it is imperative and far more effective to use a higher CCT that is nearer the color of natural daylight. Cool-white fluorescent lighting has a CCT of 4,100K, which is very good for working under and is usually the standard bulb in the circular 'daylight' desk lamps. Even better, though, are the fluorescent daylight tubes omitting a bluish-white light that are available with a CCT of 6,500K.

LIGHT POSITIONING

Setting up the optimum positioning of lighting is quite a logical – and relatively inexpensive – process. The primary objective is for your work to be well lit from all angles so that no shadows are cast over it. You need a light above and behind you and also light emitting from the left and right of you. It is also of great value to have a magnifying daylight lamp attached to your workbench. This can be used effectively by moving it around and over your work, casting shadows across its surface to help expose any scratches, uneven areas or other imperfections that need further attention.

Another very efficient way of introducing brighter and more consistent lighting in your work area is to paint the walls and ceiling white. This will dramatically enhance the light diffusion, reflecting it effectively throughout the room.

TIP If you intend to use the 6,500K strip lights and tubes, they do not necessarily have to be wired into the main wiring system of your home. A core flex can be added to the strip light with a plug on the end to insert into a wall socket. However, this must conform to your country's electrical safety standards, so consult a qualified electrician.

This filtration system cleans the air to 0.4 microns. It is ideal to place on or near your bench while you sand.

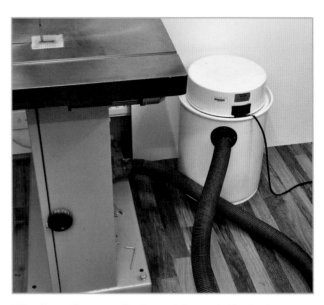

This collector filters very fine dust and also wood chips, but is purpose-made to attach to machinery via a hose.

Dust collection

Woodcarving, by its very nature, creates a high level of dust, which is obviously a health hazard, so it has to be managed carefully to ensure you have a safe environment in which to work.

There are special air-filtration systems available for workshops that filter both large and very fine airborne dust particles down to an incredible 0.4 microns. These can be wall mounted, suspended from the ceiling or standalone, wherever you wish to place them. The sizes of the units are measured by the room volume and air movement, typically in cubic meters per hour, which gives you a guide as to the appropriate unit for the size of your workspace.

If you are going to be using machinery such as a bandsaw or powered sander in your workshop, it is crucial that you also invest in an appropriate collector specifically designed for them that can handle fine dust and chippings. These are attached to the machine with a hose that sucks all the dust through a filtration system. Unfortunately, an awful lot of airborne dust is still created even when using the machine collector, so, to filter the flow of air in your working environment effectively and safely, a workshop air-filtration system and machine-dust collector should be used in combination with one another when operating your machinery.

As a final word on respiratory health, you should always wear a good-quality dust mask or respirator when sanding or using any woodworking machinery. There are three levels of mask that give protection against fine dust, graded FFP1, FFP2 and FFP3, the latter giving the highest level of protection, four times greater than the FFP2. When buying masks, always check that they conform to respiratory-mask standards for your part of the world (in the US look for NIOSH N95) and purchase either the FFP2 or the FFP3 – preferably, if you wear glasses, the design with the vent on the side of the mask (shown opposite), which is less likely to fog up your lenses.

Other workshop equipment

Here, in order of priority, is a list of other equipment that you can introduce to your workshop as and when your budget allows:

Bandsaw – buy a good-quality model with at least an 8–10in (200–250mm) cutting depth and roller-bearing guides
Flexible-shaft machine – a power carving tool (see page 20 for details)
Honing machine – for deburring and polishing tools (see page 41 for details)

This FFP2 dust mask has a vent on the side of it that directs your warm breath away from your glasses, making them less likely to mist up.

Sanding machine – for grinding and sharpening (see page 41 for details)
Battery drill/driver
Drill press
Hand drill
Clamps of various sizes
Arbotech Industrial Woodcarver – for stock removal of wood on larger projects

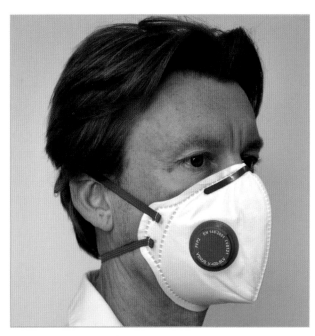

Other equipment from left to right: battery drill/driver (back); selection of clamps, including quick-grip/release, G-clamp and F-clamp (front); Arbotech industrial rotary carving blade (back); Creusen/Koch honing system (middle); and electric hand drill (front).

SHARPENING

KEEPING YOUR TOOLS SHARPENED TO A RAZOR EDGE IS A FUNDAMENTAL SKILL THAT EVERY WOODCARVER HAS TO LEARN AND PRACTICE FROM THE VERY MOMENT THAT THEY START CARVING IN ORDER TO WORK EFFICIENTLY, SAFELY AND EXTRACT THE FULL PLEASURE FROM THE SUBJECT. IT CAN TAKE A LITTLE WHILE TO BECOME FULLY ACCOMPLISHED WITH THE TECHNIQUES BUT CONSISTENT PRACTICE WILL SOON BRING YOU IMPROVED RESULTS.

When to sharpen

A razor-sharp chisel or gouge should cut smoothly through the wood without tearing the grain, leaving a shiny, smooth groove from its cutting edge, as demonstrated by the middle gouge cut seen in the picture below. The gouge cut on the right has been made with a completely blunt tool, which has had to be forced through the wood and has consequently torn the grain badly. If you study the gouge cut on the left closely, you will also notice that there are two small streaks of torn grain along the center of the cut where the cutting edge of the tool is blunt or has nicks on it. The top-right edge is also blunt or damaged, as you can see it has ripped through the grain on the right of the cut. If your tools show any signs of these imperfections when you attempt to use them, then they will need to be completely reset.

GOLDEN RULE 'Make them sharp, and keep them sharp.' When you have set up your chisels and gouges – meaning, when you have sharpened, deburred and polished them – you just need to keep them regularly stropped on a large flat strop with slip strops, giving them 10 strokes on each side to keep their edges keen. This should be performed routinely, after roughly every 10–15 minutes of hard use or as soon as you feel the edge of the tool slipping, even slightly. By doing this you will keep a razor-sharp edge for a very long time.

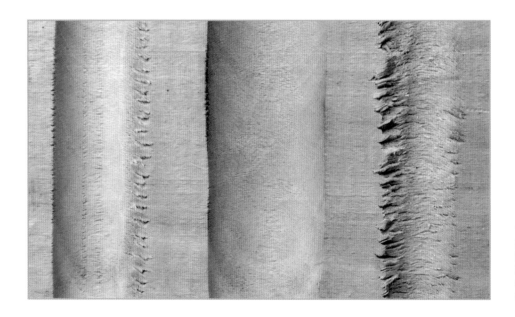

The gouge cut in the middle has been made with a razor-sharp tool, the other two gouge cuts have been made with tools that are in desperate need of sharpening.

Tools illustrating three types of incorrect sharpening, from left to right: wavy edge, bull-nosed and horned. The tool on the far right is perfectly set up.

The gouge on the right of the picture above shows a precisely set-up tool, with a flat, level cutting edge perpendicular to the sides of the tool. The three other gouges here demonstrate the three types of incorrect sharpening or honing:

1   The tool on the left has a wavy edge, which would suggest that it has either been damaged and set up incorrectly or just unevenly sharpened over a long period of time.

2   The tool second from left has the center of the cutting edge projecting much further than its sides. This is because the tool has been rocked too far when being sharpened, removing too much metal on the edges and creating this contoured, bull-nosed projection on the center of the cutting edge.

3   The tool second from right has the opposite problem: it has not been rocked far enough up to the sides, which has created uneven wear in the middle of the cutting edge and produced horns on either side.

If any of your tools have any of these issues, then they will also need to be completely reset.

The theory

All carving chisels and gouges need to have an outer bevel set on their cutting edge. The bevel is essentially the bottom edge of the blade that has been tapered down at an angle of 17–25 degrees, depending on the sweep and size of the tool, to the cutting edge, which guides the blade into the wood at a comfortable working angle to produce the cut (see the example on page 37, picture 6). For the bevel to be effective in its cut, its angled end should be ground completely flat so that it cuts evenly into the wood and can be used with ease of directional maneuverability. If the bevel were ground rounded (convex), then it would alter the angle of the cut, requiring the carver to use the tool in a higher, less directional and comfortable position. If it were ground hollow (concave), then this would weaken the cutting edge and cause the cut to dig into the wood instead of slicing evenly through it.

An inner bevel on the upper side of the cutting edge is optional – some believe it provides greater tool control – and should be set between 5–10 degrees. The two outer edges of the blade need to be perpendicular to the cutting edge of the blade, thus giving you the ability to cut cleanly into angled corners.

A selection of different bench stones, including combination (left three), Arkansas Medium, Arkansas Fine, Diamond Coarse, Small Arkansas Fine and Carborundum Oil.

Methods of sharpening

There are many different methods for sharpening your tools, but ultimately they fall into three categories:

1 Sharpening by hand with stones and strops

2 Sharpening using powered sharpening devices

3 Sharpening on a grinder and then finishing on stones and strops

In this chapter we will be looking at the first two methods, as the third is a combination of the first two.

TIP If you have any old chisels, gouges or knives with which you can practice, then work through this guide with them first to gain some experience. When you need to sharpen your new ones, you will be more knowledgeable and confident.

SHARPENING WITH STONES

This is the traditional way to sharpen your chisels. It is quite challenging to perfect and very slow, but as with every craftsmanship skill, the more you practice, the quicker you will advance.

Bench stones

Bench stones are available in a wide range of grits – you will need two, one coarse and one fine – and a variety of materials, including Arkansas oil stones, carborundum oil stones, Japanese water stones, ceramic stones and diamond whetstones. The diamond stones have become far more popular and slightly cheaper in recent years – they are very efficient and somewhat quicker to use. The Arkansas stones are also very good, especially the fine finishing stone, but be careful not to drop them, as they are brittle and break rather easily.

Be sure that you are using the correct lubrication for the type of stones that you buy, as putting oil on a water stone could ruin it. Also, some diamond stones use a base metal that will rust if you do not dry them immediately after use.

A selection of different-shaped slip stones for polishing the upper side of the blades.

Slip stones

Slip stones are also available in various materials, but again, the Arkansas ones are exceptionally effective. Fine slip stones are used to polish the flute (inside/upper side of the tool) and to help to raise the burr on the cutting edge.

STROPS

Stropping is the final part of the sharpening procedure, when you burnish the metal until the cutting edge is completely free of burrs and has a polished mirror finish. This procedure has to be applied to the bevel on the underside of the tool and the flute on the upper side.

You will need to make a flat leather strop for yourself. This is done simply by gluing a strip of thin leather, suede side up, onto a block of wood, approximately 12 x 8in (300 x 200mm). You will also need to make a small selection of slip strops for burnishing the flutes of your gouges. These can be made with any offcuts of wood, with the ends

A selection of different-shaped slip strops for burnishing the upper side of the blades and the main strop and strop dressing, for burnishing and deburring the outer bevels.

shaped to a radius that will fit inside the flutes. A piece of leather is cut to size and glued onto these curved ends. The leather will then need to be dressed with a strop dressing, which is a very fine abrasive paste or soap that removes the fine scratches from the metal, leaving a highly polished finish.

It is important to ensure that the leather you use for your strop is quite thin, around 1/16in (1–2mm). Thicker leather creates a cushioned effect when the tool is pressed onto it and is therefore more prone to wearing the edges off your tools over time, leaving a bull-nosed edge that will need to be reground square.

1

Hand sharpening techniques

Described below are the techniques required for sharpening the key tools you will be using in this book.

GOUGES: SWEEPS NO. 2–NO. 11

1   First, if the edge of your gouge is uneven or damaged, it will need to be reshaped to a square edge. Hold the tool at a 90-degree vertical position on the coarse stone and rub it back and forth along the entire length of the stone until the cutting edge is perfectly flat and square to the edges. Ideally this should be accomplished on a grinding wheel if you have one, but be very careful not to burn the metal.

2   To create the bevel on the underside of your gouge, carefully hold it at an angle of about 20 degrees (**2a**) and horizontally rock it from corner to corner evenly along the full length of the stone (**2b**), being careful to maintain the correct angle. After every minute or so, check the bevel underneath to make sure that you are reaching both edges of the gouge and achieving a

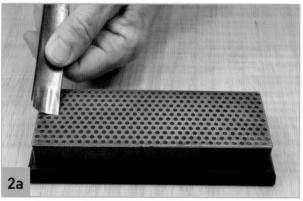

2a

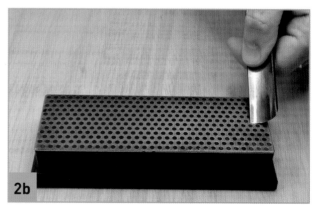

2b

uniform level. Remember not to rock it too far or you will remove too much metal from the side edges (see gouge 2 on page 33, for example).

3   Continue this process until you have ground the bevel evenly up to the cutting edge of the blade and produced a small, wafer-thin burr. Inspect the edge of the tool to make sure that the cutting edge is perfectly square and make adjustments if necessary.

4   Next, use a fine slip stone to polish the inside edge of the flute. Lay your gouge on the bench and, using a suitably shaped slip stone, place it in the flute of the gouge and rub it backwards and forwards, moving it across the radius. This will polish the flute and continue to raise the burr on this inner edge. Repeat steps 2–4 using the 'fine' bench stone to polish the 'coarse' stone scratches along the outer bevel, which should then raise and remove most of the burr from the cutting edge.

5   Next you need to burnish the sharpened tool. Burnishing – polishing a surface by friction – can be used on many different mediums, including wood, paper, metal and clay. When it comes to sharpening tools, it means to polish the beveled cutting edge and flute of the chisel or gouge by using dressed leather strops. Start by holding the gouge on the dressed leather at the correct angle on the left corner then draw it towards you, slowly rocking it over to the right corner in one full length of the strop. Repeat the process, this time starting on the right corner and rocking it over to the left as you draw it towards you. Keep alternating so that you maintain even wear along the edge. Repeat until the beveled edge has a mirror finish. Next burnish the inner edge of the flute. Choose a slip strop with a suitable radius and work it in one direction, outwards over the cutting edge. Do not try to rub it back into the flute, as the edge of the gouge will slice into the leather.

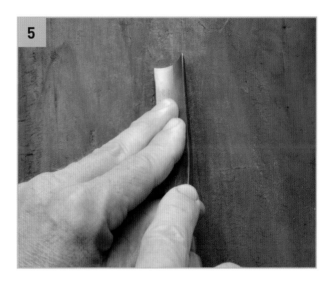

6   By now, any remaining burr should have been removed, leaving a mirror polished, perfectly set-up, razor-sharp tool.

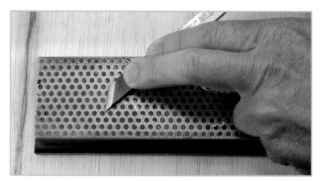

FLAT CHISEL NO. 1 (FLAT) AND NO. 1S (SKEW)

The No. 1 and No. 1S each have bevels on both sides of the blade and, although held at different angles, they are sharpened using the same techniques. The No. 1 is held on the angle of its bevel, square on the coarse stone, and rubbed up and down evenly on both sides of the blade until the burr is formed (see above left). This is repeated on the fine stone to polish the scratches

from the coarse stone and further raise the burr before burnishing it on the flat strop to polish the bevels and completely deburr them. The same procedure is used for the No. 1S (see above right) but it is held at an angle of about 45 degrees to keep the cutting edge parallel on the stone. Be sure to keep an even pressure along the cutting edge so that the tip does not become uneven.

V-TOOL NO. 12

The V-Tool is by far the most challenging tool to sharpen because of its complex anatomy. In effect, it has three cutting edges and should be sharpened as two flat No. 1 chisels (one on each side of the tool) and a tiny gouge in the center. The keel at the base of the V-Tool is actually rounded like a very small gouge and not a sharp angle. This cutting edge has to be curved so that it can slice through the wood smoothly and evenly; if it were sharpened to a point, then at best it would just tear through the grain of the wood and be of no use whatsoever.

1   Starting with the coarse stone again, if necessary square off the cutting edge first.

2   Sharpen the two flat edges of the blade using the same method as outlined for the No. 1 chisel (see above): hold each side in turn flat on the angle of its bevel and rub it up and down the full length of the coarse stone until a burr is formed (**2a**), (**2b**).

3   At this point you may notice that a small 'beak' has formed on the keel. This is expected and occurs because the metal at the base of the keel is a lot thicker than at the shoulders of the tool.

4   Before you start work on the keel, study picture 7 on page 40 to see how far the bevel at the base of the keel extends back in relation to the two straight edges; it is almost twice as far! This is very important to establish correctly, so that the tool can be used effectively at a comfortable, low angle. Work on this area of the keel next then, by horizontally rocking it evenly from side to side (**4a**), (**4b**), (**4c**), in the same method as described for the gouges (see steps 2a and 2b on page 36). Do this until you have established the correct angle of the bevel and the two straight sides and the center keel (tiny gouge) are perfectly level with each other.

5   Next use a very thin, flat, fine slip stone that fits comfortably into the inside of the blade to polish the cutting edges of the blade and to raise the burr here. Repeat steps 2–5 using the 'fine' bench stone.

6 Finally, polish the inside of the blade with a tiny, flat, slip strop (**6a**) and then burnish the outer bevels of all three sides of the cutting edge (**6b**), bringing them up to a fine, razor-sharp, mirror-polished finish.

7 Here is the finished V-Tool showing the correctly set, flat beveled square edge with the rounded extended keel.

TIP When stropping the V-Tool, strop the keel twice as much as the two flat sides. This keeps the wear even, preventing the 'beak' from forming and saving the trouble of having to reset the tool again as frequently.

KNIVES

A knife should very rarely need to be reground, as regularly stropping its very fine blade should keep it in a perfect razor-sharp state. But there is always the chance, of course, that you might accidentally damage it on the edge of your metal faceplate or in some other way, or the blade may become uneven in its wear over time.

If the edge needs to be reshaped, then start on a coarse or medium stone, holding it at an angle of just a few degrees, and work both sides of the blade evenly until a burr is formed (see picture below). Swap to a fine or ultra-fine stone and repeat the process. It can then be burnished on your flat strop to remove the fine scratches left from the stone and any remaining burr, bringing it back up to a polished sharp edge. If the edge is not too badly damaged and it doesn't need to be reshaped, then you should be able to sharpen it effectively using just the fine stone and strop.

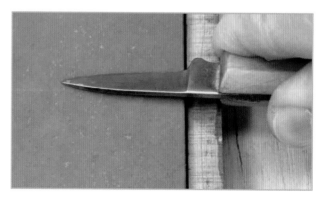

Powered sharpening

There are many different devices available today that are used to quickly and efficiently bring your blunted or damaged tool up to a fine polished finish. These fall into two main categories: grinding and polishing. The grinding machines include whetstones, dry grinders and belt sanders, which are used to straighten the cutting edge and reset the bevel. The polishing machines are generally a motorized unit with two wheels made of various materials including leather and felt, which de-burr the cutting edge and polish the bevel and inner flute.

GRINDING

In the example below, a belt sander is being used with a clean 120-grit belt, which quickly squares the cutting edge and re-sets the bevel. The gouge is held at an angle of approximately 20 degrees and then slowly rocked from side to side across the full width of the sanding belt to keep the frictional heat as low as possible. As the burr is forming, it becomes easier to see how level the edge is being ground, which can then be further worked on any areas that may be uneven. When the angle of the bevel is set and the cutting edge is level with the burr raised, then the grinding is complete and it is ready to be polished.

POLISHING

All polishing wheels must first be dressed with a very fine abrasive, which is usually sold in the form of a solid block known as 'soap.'

1   In this example, a honing machine fitted with felt wheels is being used to polish and de-burr the cutting edge of a gouge. The gouge is held firmly at the correct angle of 20 degrees and evenly rocked from side to side over the surface of the wheel. As the friction between the gouge and the felt wheel heats up, the soap liquefies and its abrasive qualities polish the ground beveled edge and further raise the burr.

2   The lower edge of the flute is then polished but held level against the wheel and moved just around its outer edges. This causes the burr to flake away and creates a mirror-polished, razor-sharp edge that is ready for use. It is important to note, however, that due to the tighter curvature of the sweeps No. 8 to No. 12, it is impossible to polish their inner flutes on the wheels, so they have to be finished by hand using slip strops.

FURTHERING YOUR KNOWLEDGE ON SHARPENING

Unfortunately there is only room in this book to summarize some of the basic fundamental principles and techniques of sharpening, but there are some excellent publications available that comprehensively examine the subject in detail, several of which I have listed in the bibliography on page 193.

WOOD

WOOD IS A FABULOUS MEDIUM IN WHICH TO WORK, WITH SO MANY SPECIES TO CHOOSE FROM AND VARIATIONS OF COLOR TONES AND GRAIN FIGURING TO USE WITHIN A DESIGN. WOOD IS A LIVING MEDIUM WITH A COMPLEX STRUCTURE OF VARIABLES IN THE WAY THAT IT MATURES AND GROWS. IT IS IMPORTANT TO LEARN A LITTLE ABOUT ITS GROWTH CYCLE, HOW IT IS CUT, PREPARED AND DRIED AND, MOST IMPORTANTLY, WHAT TO BE AWARE OF WHEN SELECTING A PIECE FOR CARVING.

The anatomy of a tree trunk

A tree trunk is composed of five different layers:

1   The outer bark (rhytidome) is the exterior crust of the tree, which is the layer that protects it from the elements. This outer cork layer is actually dead but is continually renewed from the inner bark, the phloem.

2   The inner bark (phloem) is like an aqueduct of live tissues with tubular cells that transport the vital food made by the leaves down the trunk to feed other parts of the tree. It only lives for a short time and then dies and becomes part of the protective layer of the outer bark.

3   The cambium, which is positioned between the phloem and the sapwood, is like a tissue or membrane of dividing cells that create the new growth of the wood, the annual growth rings.

4   The sapwood (alburnum) is the lighter-colored wood between the bark and the heartwood, which acts as a conduit to transport the sap (liquids, vital minerals and food from other storage cells) up the tree to the leaves. It has lighter-colored annual growth rings than the heartwood, with larger pores for the transportation of the liquids. When the annual growth rings of sapwood mature, they lose their vitality and become part of the dead heartwood.

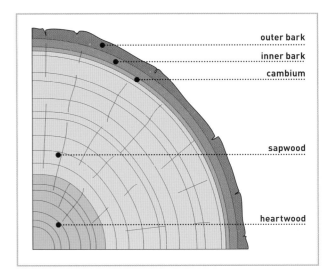

outer bark
inner bark
cambium
sapwood
heartwood

5   The heartwood (duramen) is the strong center of the tree. It is darker in color and comprised of the dead cell structures of the annual growth rings, which are used for storage.

TIP   It is a good idea to familiarize yourself with the medium so that you understand the section or cut of lumber you are using for your projects. There is no better way to do this than to take a trip to a local saw mill that is specifically producing lumber for carving, turning or furniture, where you will be able to talk to experts about its growth and production, and see the various procedures for cutting and drying the lumber.

Hardwood and softwood

The distinction between hardwood and softwood is that hardwood trees are angiosperms, which are broad-leaved trees whose seeds have an ovary or shell – apple, pear, oak, walnut and chestnut, for example. Softwood trees, such as the conifers and cycads, are gymnosperms whose seeds are found naked without an ovary or shell casing, such as the cones that are dropped from these species of trees. Hardwoods and softwoods are sometimes confused: a classic example is balsa wood, which is actually a hardwood, while the extremely hard yew is a softwood.

Quarter-sawn lumber: very stable and less inclined to bow, twist, cup or warp.

Planking methods

The two main methods for cutting planks are quarter sawn and plain sawn.

QUARTER SAWN

Quarter-sawn boards are cut in a radial method, first by sectioning the tree trunk into quarters and then cutting the quarters into separate boards, each one being cut perpendicular to the annual growth rings. Boards cut this way have a higher level of stability than plain-sawn boards both when drying and when dry, and because of the orientation of the growth rings, they are less inclined to bow, twist, cup or warp. Unfortunately it is becoming much harder to find quarter-sawn lumber now, as it is more labor intensive to produce, generates more waste and is not as cost-effective to produce as plain-sawn wood. If you are fortunate enough to locate some, be prepared to pay a premium price for it.

PLAIN SAWN

Plain-sawn boards are cut tangentially in parallel lengths through the tree. This method is far more straightforward than quarter sawn – faster, less labor intensive and produces very little, if any, waste – making it the most cost-effective to produce and

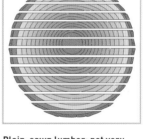

Plain-sawn lumber: not very stable and prone to bow, twist, cup and warp.

cheaper to purchase. However, when cut in this way, it creates uneven drying through the boards, which causes the wood to bow, cup, twist and warp. Shrinkage is also more of a problem than the radial-cut quarter-sawn method, both in thickness and width. It is worth knowing that planks cut either side of the exact center of the tree are, in fact, true quarter-sawn boards because of the orientation of the growth rings here. These should be sought after or requested when buying your wood for carving.

Drying methods

It is advisable, especially for the beginner, to buy seasoned (dried) wood as opposed to green (freshly cut or still wet) lumber, which needs to be dried correctly so that it does not develop any checks (cracks or splits). There are two ways in which lumber is dried after it has been cut and planked – either air dried or kiln dried.

AIR DRIED (AD)

Air-dried lumber is, or should be, dried under cover to protect it from the dampness of the rain and the direct sunlight. The wood is cut into planks and then stickered, as it is called, each plank being layered horizontally one on top of the other and separated with a small strip of softwood of around ½ x 2in (13 x 50mm), called a sticker, laid across the boards. This allows the air to circulate around the stack, preventing any mold from forming and enabling the boards to dry out slowly. The rule of thumb for air drying is that for each inch (25mm) of thickness, the board should be left to dry for approximately one year.

KILN DRIED (KD)

Kiln drying is the artificial process of drying wood in an enclosed environment by means of a controlled atmosphere (temperature, humidity and ventilation) until the wood reaches a predetermined moisture content of between 6 and 8 per cent. This method of drying wood is extremely efficient and dramatically reduces the drying time to weeks or months rather than years like the AD method.

Moisture content (MC)

Wood is hygroscopic, which means that it absorbs and releases moisture to balance itself in relation to the moisture or humidity of its surrounding environment, even after it has been fully seasoned. In effect, this means that the wood will shrink when it releases moisture but swell again when

A moisture meter is being used here to check the moisture content of a piece of walnut. It is reading 10%, which is dry enough to bring into a centrally heated environment without the risk of developing checks.

it absorbs it, and as it shrinks and swells, it is liable to warp and check. So some consideration must always be given when transferring your wood from one environment to another.

The MC of the wood that you purchase is a very important factor that you must be aware of before bringing it into your workshop or centrally heated home. If the wood has not been left to dry for long enough, and the MC is not low enough, then the humidity and temperature inside your workshop or house could cause the moisture left inside the wood to escape too rapidly in an uncontrolled manner, which would very likely cause checks to develop rather quickly. The MC of fully seasoned AD lumber in temperate climates in summer is around 12–14 per cent, which is adequate for indoor use, but if the MC is 18 per cent or over then it could be a problem. On the other hand, at 6–8 per cent, the MC of KD wood is substantially lower than that of AD wood, which makes it completely stable and it won't check.

There are several ways to measure the MC of wood, but the quickest and most convenient way is with a moisture meter. When you are purchasing a block or plank of wood, rather than leaving it to chance, ask the salesperson to check the MC reading for you at several positions on the plank, so that you know exactly what you are dealing with.

Most species of wood, whether hard or soft, can be carved to some degree, but hardwood is generally accepted as the first choice. The most appropriate of these hardwoods are the fruit woods, including lime (also called basswood or linden), walnut, cherry, plum, apple and pear, which are all slow growers, have tight annual growth rings and are excellent for carving. From an ecological angle, it is important to purchase lumber from reputable, sustainable sources.

SELECTING GOOD LUMBER

Lumber for woodcarving is sold either in small, prepared carving blanks or by the board. It is most commonly available in thicknesses of between 1–4in (25–100mm), occasionally 5–6in (125–150mm), and of varying widths and lengths. The heartwood is generally sought after for carving, but a combination of the heartwood and sapwood can be used to great effect to add interesting color contrasts and realistic effects to the projects, as demonstrated in the Emperor Penguin, Humpback Whale and Cat projects in this book.

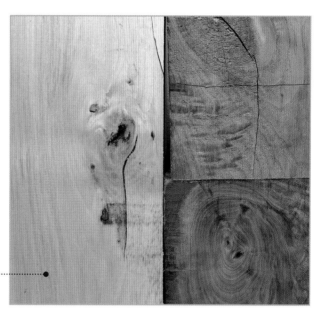

Here is a selection of wood that is absolutely useless for woodcarving. The piece of lime on the left has blue discoloration in the grain from moisture contamination when drying, which makes the wood very brittle and nasty to carve. All three pieces have large knots, which cause the surrounding grain to become eccentric in its direction and impossible to carve unless using power carving tools. The lime and top piece of black walnut both have checks, possibly from the presence of knots, but also because of the drying method used.

This selection has all of the good qualities that should be sought after in a piece of lumber for carving: good, tight, even, close grain running consistently up through the boards, with no knots, checks or discoloration – and there will be no waste.

Wood for carving

1 Apple fairly hard; prone to checks; takes fine detail

2 Beech hard; not for the beginner; takes detail (pictured: American beech)

3 Birch quite hard; carves cleanly; takes fine detail (pictured: paper birch)

4 Butternut soft and easy to carve; widely used in the USA; takes fine detail

5 Cherry fairly hard; excellent carving properties; takes fine detail (pictured: American cherry)

6 Chestnut (horse) hard; not for the beginner; takes detail if carved carefully

7 Chestnut (sweet) hard; good carving qualities; takes fine detail

8 Holly hard and unstable; good carving qualities; takes fine detail

9 Hornbeam medium hard; not for the beginner; takes detail (pictured: European hornbeam)

10 Lime (basswood) soft to medium; excellent carving qualities for beginners; takes fine detail

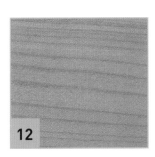

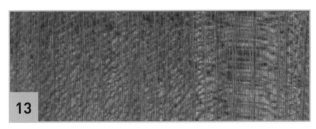

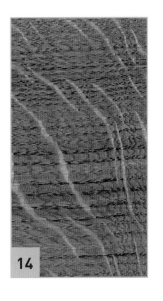

11 London plane (lacewood) hard; similar to lime; takes good detail

12 Magnolia medium hard; similar to lime; takes fine detail

13 Mulberry medium hard; easy to carve; takes fine detail

14 Oak (European) hard; good for outdoor carvings; takes detail

15 Oak (red American) hard; good for outdoor carvings; takes detail

16 Olivewood hard; close grain; good carving qualities; takes fine detail

17 Pear medium hard; unstable and prone to checks but excellent carving qualities; takes fine detail

18 Plum medium hard; unstable and prone to checks; takes fine detail

19 Tulipwood medium; good carving qualities similar to lime; takes fine detail (pictured: Brazilian tulipwood)

20 Walnut (European) hard; excellent carving qualities; takes fine detail

21 Walnut (American black) hard; excellent carving qualities; takes fine detail

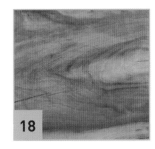

Choosing the right woods for the beginner

One of the aims here is to build your confidence and facilitate quick and effective progress by suggesting wood that is relatively easy to work with. This will help to make your first experience of carving a positive and enjoyable one. In turn, I hope it will stimulate your enthusiasm for the subject and inspire you, giving you the desire to develop and advance your practical, technical and creative skills. To this end, lime wood is a great introduction to carving, as it is very easy to carve and especially forgiving when carved against the grain. It also takes very fine detail and has a porcelain-like elegance when bleached.

Once you have produced your first couple of carvings in lime, you will have learned some of the important and fundamental techniques of working with the medium in three dimensions, which should give you the experience and confidence to progress onto a more challenging subject and material. When you reach this stage, either American black walnut or English cherry are great second steps, both of which are much more dense than lime and a lot less forgiving when carving close to the grain. This will further the development of your technical skills and give you a deeper understanding and practical experience of the grain direction and how to approach it. They are also far more attractive than lime and look beautiful when oiled and wax polished – which justifies the extra energy and time that it takes to work with them.

An even-colored and figured piece of lumber is more appropriate for projects such as a human bust, which will enhance the details of the face and its surface anatomy.

Choosing the right woods for the subject

When choosing an appropriate species of wood for your project, some consideration must always be given to the subject that you are carving. For example, if you are carving a bust, then the facial features and hair will be far more effective if you use an even-colored, even-figured and even-grained wood, regardless of whether it is light (lime) or dark (walnut). This will enhance the details of the face and subtle surface anatomy in a much more realistic and defined way. If a highly figured piece of walnut were used for such a subject, then the figuring of the wood would become the main point of focus when viewed, so taking the eye away from the carved detail, distorting or losing the facial features that you have tried so hard to portray accurately and potentially ruining the impact and effect of the finished piece.

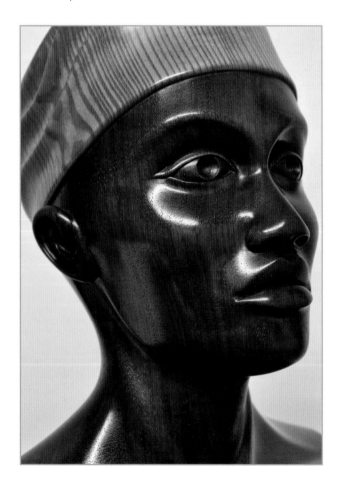

A highly figured piece of lumber or a burr will lend its grain structure beautifully to enhance the visual impact of an abstract sculpture.

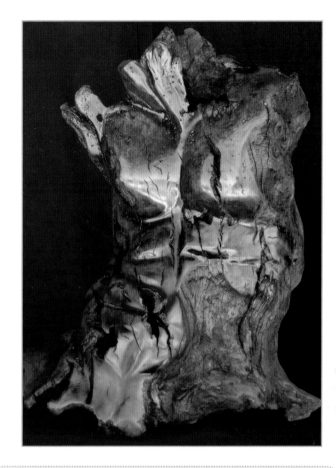

Conversely, if you are making an abstract sculpture with undefined detail, piercings, large planes and subtle contours, then a highly figured piece of wood will lend its properties beautifully to the sculpture and really enhance the impact of the finished piece.

Top-ten carving woods for the beginner
1 **Lime** (basswood)
2 **Butternut** (popular in North America but rare elsewhere)
3 **American black walnut**
4 **Cherry**
5 **European walnut**
6 **Tulipwood**
7 **Pear**
8 **Apple**
9 **Sweet chestnut**
10 **London plane**

Here is a checklist for you to refer to when buying your wood:

- Ensure that the wood you purchase is from a reputable and sustainable source.

- Try to buy quarter-sawn lumber if available and affordable.

- If you are buying a plank, inspect the ends of the board for checks and see how far they go up the board. Up to 6in (150mm) is acceptable and considered as waste, but if they continue up through the board, then move on and check the next one.

- If there is a choice, then don't buy the original end of the plank; try to select the center board if there is one available.

- Sight down the length of the board to see if it is badly warped. If this is so, you could be shaving off a substantial amount of the thickness to reach a perfectly planed flat surface, which is necessary for bandsawing.

- Check for woodworm – they love walnut especially – and if you see small, regular-sized holes, avoid like the plague.

- Knots, checks and splits all lead to a lot of useless wasted wood.

- Blue staining in the grain means water contamination, which renders the wood nasty to carve.

- Look for a tight, close grain that runs consistently all the way along the length of the board.

- When you find a good piece, ask the salesperson to check the MC reading for you.

USING WOODCARVING TOOLS

THERE ARE COUNTLESS TOOL TECHNIQUES AND VARIATIONS THEREOF THAT YOU NEED TO LEARN IN ORDER TO PRODUCE THE FINE DETAILS AND SUBTLE CONTOURS OF THREE-DIMENSIONAL WORK, BUT YOU MUST FIRST START WITH THE BASIC PRINCIPLES OF GRIP, BALANCE, CONTROL AND SAFETY. IT WOULD BE OF GREAT BENEFIT TO EXPERIMENT WITH THE TECHNIQUES DISCUSSED IN THIS CHAPTER AND GAIN SOME EXPERIENCE BEFORE ATTEMPTING THE PROJECTS.

The fundamental purpose of the chisels and gouges that we use for woodcarving is to cut into dense, hard wood, and they have to be razor sharp to do this. If one of these tools were to accidentally slip into any part of your body when in use, it would slice through your skin and muscle like a hot knife through butter.

Cutting yourself while carving is the last thing that anyone wants to happen, so if you adopt the following rules into your code of good practice, then you should never cut yourself.

- Whenever possible, always secure your work safely in a vise or with clamps, leaving both hands free to hold the tools.

- Never attempt to carve one-handed unless you are using a mallet as the accelerator.

- Never cut towards any part of your body and keep both hands behind the direction of the cut.

- If you are right handed, always rest part of your left hand or fingers on the wood for safety and to aid your balance and control. If you are left handed, then do the opposite.

- Always place your tools safely back on your bench after use, with the cutting edge facing forwards.

- Never wander around with your tools.

- Never gesticulate or wave your tools around when you are talking.

- Always keep your tools razor sharp, so that they can be used with less pressure. A sharp tool is far less likely to slip than a blunt one.

- Always take great care and be very focused when you are taking tools out or putting them back into your tool roll.

- Be aware that No. 12s (V-Tools) and knives are the most dangerous to use, as they have a tendency to run or slip. They should be used with great care.

- Never take any risks, and if you hear your inner voice warning you, or sense danger in what you are doing, then simply just stop.

Carving one-handed and towards your body are two extremely dangerous practices that should be avoided at all costs.

The sculpture is securely fastened to the vise leaving both hands free to work safely and accurately around it. Both hands are behind the cutting direction of the blade, eliminating any possibility of injury.

The picture on the right clearly shows the correct, orthodox method of grip with both hands holding the gouge and working in a safe direction of cut. If for any reason the tool were to slip, there is no chance that it could do any injury to the carver, as no part of the body is in front of the direction of pressure and the cutting edge of the blade.

All of these safety tips are quite obvious and logical really, but please do take heed of them and adopt a good code of safety into your carving techniques right from day one – they will very quickly become second nature to you. By doing this, you will eliminate any chance of injury to yourself or to the other people around you.

HAND-HELD SAFETY

There will be occasions when you have to carve something hand-held because it is impossible to secure the wood in a way that allows you access to work on it properly. This is far from ideal, but, again, if you follow these simple rules carefully, then you will not have a problem. You will find visual references to accompany the techniques outlined for safe hand-held carving in the Humpback Whale project on page 185.

- Never carve in the direction of your fingers or hands.

- Make sure that your tools are razor sharp to eliminate any chance of them slipping.

- Hold the gouges in the same way as you would a pencil, roughly 1in (25mm) away from the cutting edge.

- Always try to have your ring finger (right hand) touching the wood to help give you good balance and control – better still, your little finger as well if possible.

- Make very shallow cuts so that the tool slices through the wood easily and you are not straining your fingers with the pressure. This helps avoid any chance of the tool slipping.

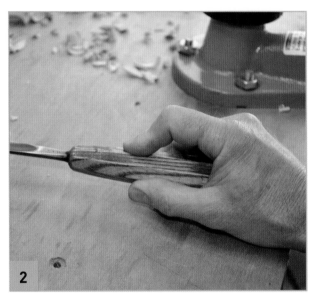

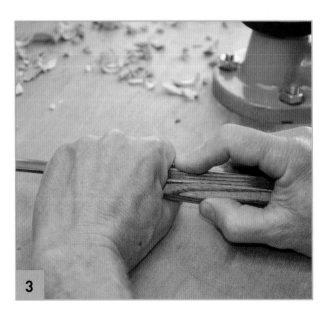

Developing your own style

Our anatomies vary considerably from person to person, including the size and shape of our fingers, hands and arms. Consequently, we all naturally develop our own way of holding and working with our tools, just as we did when we were young with our pens and pencils, and this is certainly something that should be encouraged. However, it is also very important to learn the orthodox methods from day one so that you have a good understanding of how to control tools effectively and safely.

CHISELS AND GOUGES

Using the carving tools effectively and safely comes through a balance of pressure and resistance. If you are right handed, the right hand is used to apply the force (accelerator), while the left is used to control the resistance (brake). The left hand can also be used for applying force when needed, but it is mostly this hand that stops the tool from running on.

Please note, all the steps here are described from the perspective of right-handed carvers. If you are left handed, then switch it all around.

1   To achieve the correct grip of the tool, place the end of the tool handle firmly into the palm of your right hand.

2   Naturally clasp your fingers around the handle, with your index finger pointing down towards the top flat edge of the blade. Draw your index finger back slightly by bending your middle knuckle and sliding the tip down the handle towards you.

3   Clasp your left hand around the blade of the tool with the index finger and thumb butted up against the shoulder where the blade joins the handle.

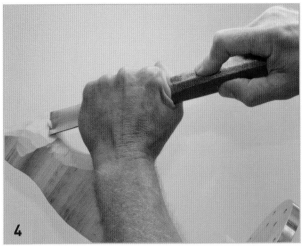

4   The right hand is used to force pressure (accelerate) into the cut, and the left wrist articulates from side to side, giving control to the cuts and applying the resistance (brake). The lower edge of your left palm, or another part of your left hand, should always be in contact with your work to aid balance and control.

5   If you are using a mallet to work with, then the left hand stays in the exact same position on the tool, while the right hand is used to deliver the blows from the mallet.

KNIVES

The knife is an extremely versatile and important tool to learn to use, and one that you should take up at the start of your learning. The correct grip is to hold the knife in the same way as you would a pen or pencil, so that you can direct the cutting tip in a controlled manner along the detail as you do when you write or draw. The ring and little fingers are always kept in contact with the surface of the wood that you are carving, both for safety and to help give you better balance and control.

Knives are not the easiest of tools to master, as they have the tendency to slip under pressure. An effective technique to minimize this problem is to make an initial shallow cut along the detail to produce a tram line, which is then cut a second time but much deeper and with less risk of the blade slipping off the line of detail. It is also good practice to strop the blade frequently in between each cut on a dressed leather strop to further minimize the risk of it slipping. Ten strokes on each side are enough to keep a razor-sharp edge on it (see page 40 for more on this).

The knife is held using the same grip as you would a pencil, which will give you maximum control of directional use.

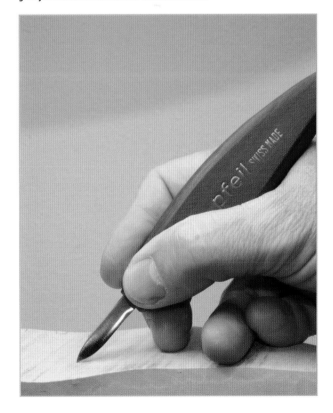

There are two areas of detail work where the knife is most prone to slipping. The first is as you approach the edge of the wood. An example of this would be the tail feathers of the Emperor Penguin project (see page 158, picture 26). When you are creating an area of detail like this, you will need to lighten the pressure of the cut as you work towards the edge of the wood, stopping before the knife slips off the edge. Then simply reverse the cut, by pushing the blade away from you over the detail line, but using the length of the blade to make the cut rather than the tip. Alternatively, if you can, turn the carving around and start the cut gently from the edge and work inwards.

The other area to be aware of is when you are cutting a detail over a raised contour or into a hollow. Always make sure that you keep the knife blade at its primary cutting angle by lowering or raising your hand and the angle of cut in relation to the contour that you are working on. This will ensure that the edge of the blade remains safely in contact with the surface. If you bend your wrist towards you, altering the angle of the cut too high, then it can very easily slip without warning.

Carving with finesse and control

The initial roughing out of a carving or sculpture requires you to administer a huge amount of pressure into your cuts, hence the need for a firm grip. But as you take the carving onto an advanced or detailed stage, then you need to adjust your techniques so that you can work in a more refined, controlled and directional way. Generally speaking, this is the point when the woodcarver will naturally develop their individual styles to carefully work with precision over the various depths and details of their sculpture.

The techniques at this stage will vary, depending on the angle and type of detail that is being created. But the main difference is that the fingertips of the left hand are used to guide the cutting edge accurately around the piece with a more refined control. The right hand may remain in its original position but with a more relaxed grip, or the fingertips could be used to apply a more precise area of pressure.

KNIFE PRACTICE EXERCISE

Before you attempt to use a knife on your carving, find an offcut of wood with a level surface and secure it safely to your vise. Draw some straight and curved lines onto it and practice drawing the knife along them. Make the first cut shallow, then follow it through with a deeper one. When you have made your initial tram line, you can, if necessary, use your thumb or index finger from your left hand to add pressure to the blade to slice deeper. Don't forget to strop your knife ten times each side in between each line that you carve. When your confidence grows, do the same but on a curved surface. It is worth investing time in developing your knife techniques, as they can be employed for many applications, including deep-angled cuts (such as the corners of the eyes), wrinkles, deep slits, whittling, awkward-angled detail and hand-held work.

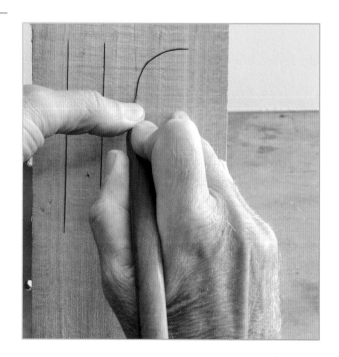

Here are a few examples of these techniques:

1   The fingertips of the left hand are used to hold the tool at 1–2in (25–50mm) away from the cutting edge, which gives far more control over the direction of cut.

2   This No. 12 (V-Tool) is being carefully guided along the design line using the thumb, index and middle fingers. The ring and little fingers are braced on the wood to support the hand safely and give balance and control to the cut.

3   The blade is being guided by the thumb, index and little finger. The hand is being supported safely by the middle and ring fingers gripping the rear edge of the sculpture, aiding control and balance to the cuts.

There are many more examples of directional carving techniques throughout the project chapters.

Bad practice

There are a number of bad habits that the beginner could easily acquire when learning without guidance, so it is important to be aware of them before you start your first project to ensure that you only adopt safe, efficient, beneficial and orthodox methods.

Most bad practices are those that are naturally developed by the learner to compensate for the fact that they are struggling to carve the wood with blunt tools. Here are a few:

• **Screwdriver**: this is the practice of twisting the wrist from side to side while pushing the tool through the grain in the same way as you would use a screwdriver. This warning is a little controversial because many tutors actually teach this method, but the reason for cautioning against it is that if your tool needs this technique to slice through the wood then it is, quite simply, not sharp enough. This technique can actually mask the fact that the tool needs to be stropped or sharpened and can very quickly become the main technique that carvers use to remove waste wood – and it is a very hard habit to break.

• **Shunting the tools**: this method of carving into the mass by rapidly pushing the tools back and forth in their own channel is a very unsophisticated and unrefined way of carving. It is painful to watch, lacks control and skill and should never be adopted.

• **Levering the tools**: never lever your tools under any circumstances because steel does not flex. If you do try to lever out a chip of wood instead of taking the time to make a crosscut then there is a high risk of snapping the cutting edge, requiring the tool to be completely set up again. Always, without exception, make sure that your tool cuts meet and the chip comes out in an orthodox manner.

• **Using your palm as a mallet**: this is another common bad habit that can seriously damage the carpal tunnel of tendons and nerves in your hand and wrist. A proper mallet is a valuable tool to have in your workshop and one that you need to learn how to use to good effect, but your delicate hands are definitely not a recommended alternative, so avoid this bad habit at all costs.

Using the palm as a mallet is a bad practice that can cause serious problems to your hands and wrists. It should never be adopted in preference to the effective use of a well-balanced mallet.

Good practice

Good practice of technical skills when carving is a combination of several elements, the principles of which are listed here:

• **Razor-sharp tools**: if your tools are properly sharp and kept sharp, they will be very effective in their performance, slicing through the grain evenly and precisely – and they will be a real joy to use.

• **Clean carving**: from the very moment that you start your first carving, you should strive to attain a high level of achievement. Clean carving is the process of working through the project in a methodical, organized manner, creating even depths and carefully finishing details one area at a time as opposed to swapping between different areas, leaving parts incomplete and unlevel or creating messy inner corners where the cuts from two different directions do not quite meet up.

• **Finesse and patience**: finesse is the art of the delicate touch in combination with close observation. It is about learning techniques that enable you to produce very fine, high-quality work and finish – whether your piece is representational or abstract – and developing the eye to balance the elements of the form and bring unity to the composition. This takes time to perfect and challenges every artist.

Always strive to carve in a methodical and clean manner, making sure that the surfaces are even in depth and that the inner-angled corner cuts join each other perfectly.

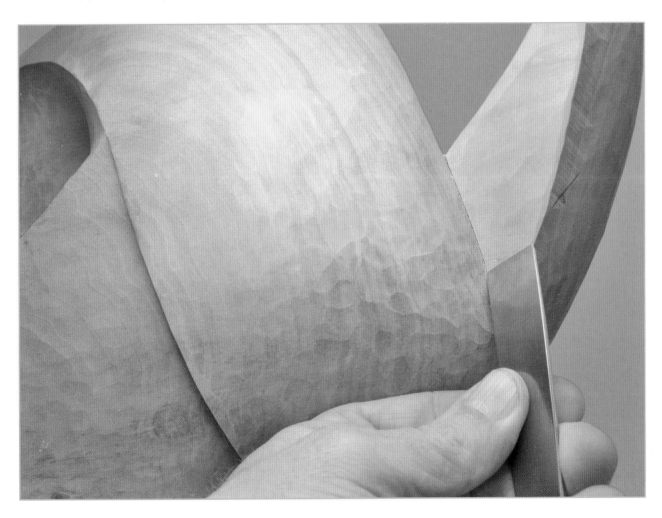

EFFECTIVE SANDING

THE SANDING OF A CARVING OR SCULPTURE IS THE FINAL PROCESS OF ITS PRODUCTION, WHICH SHAPES, SOFTENS AND BLENDS ALL OF THE DETAILS NATURALLY TOGETHER, TRANSFORMING THE MODELED SURFACE INTO LIFE. THE INTENTION HERE IS TO GUIDE YOU THROUGH THE QUICKEST AND MOST EFFICIENT TECHNIQUES AND MATERIALS THAT WILL ENSURE A SUPERB FINISH ON THE SURFACE OF YOUR WORK.

Materials

The sanding procedure is particularly labor intensive and can be quite tedious, especially around fine detail, so it is important that you use the most effective materials to accomplish the job as quickly and efficiently as possible. There is a wide range of sanding products available, and you will need to use the right combination to produce the best finish.

One of the most important qualities required from abrasives for carving purposes is a flexible composition, so that they can be folded or curved to get into awkward areas to smooth the details. They need to be able to take a fold without the material splitting or fracturing along the crease.

Cloth-backed abrasives as opposed to paper-backed ones are best in this regard. There are many brands available, but the one that I have found by far the most effective is the Hermes RB406 J-Flex, which lasts for a very long time and is extremely good to work with. This is available in grits ranging from 80 to 600, is usually sold in yard/meter lengths and is 4in (100mm) in width.

Another abrasive that I would recommend that works well in combination with the J-Flex is a product called Abranet by Mirka. This product is a significant leap forward in the development of abrasives, as it has a unique Velcro-backed webbing construction containing thousands of small holes.

Hermes RB406 J-Flex aluminium oxide abrasive sanding sheets.

Abranet strips by Mirka.

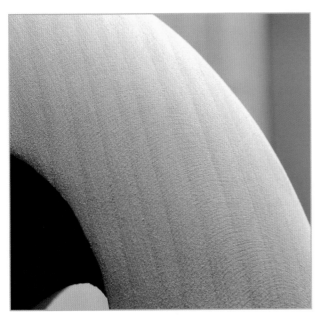

The Abranet produces an extremely even sanding pattern on the surface of the wood.

The 1,200-grit polishing discs are used to remove the minute scratches on the surface of the wood before it is finished with oil and wax polish.

The holes keep the dust off the surface of the abrasive material to prevent it clogging up so quickly and significantly reduce airborne dust particles.

Abranet is extremely effective at cutting through gouge marks and leveling uneven surfaces, leaving a uniform sanding pattern (see above left) and remains effective for an incredible length of time. However, there is one issue to be aware of when using this product: because of the way it is made, in little strips of zigzagged lines (see the middle left picture on page 64), you must always keep the direction of the sanding motion, moving from side to side and forwards and backwards, otherwise it will leave little striped lines in perfect formation on your work. Abranet is available in grits ranging from 80 to 600 and comes in various sizes, including 3 x 5in (75 x 125mm) strips in a box of 50.

The final abrasive that you will need for the finishing process is a fabric polishing disc of between 1,000–1,500, 1,200 being about perfect. This is used to remove all of the minute surface scratches left over from the initial sanding and bring the surface to a perfect polished finish. These can be folded into all kinds of shapes and are a pleasure to use. However, you will need to be very careful when sanding over

vulnerable details such as fingers, working in one direction over the sharp edge, so as to eliminate any chance of the fabric snagging on the detail and breaking it. These discs are available from 400–4,000-grit, and the products I would recommend include Festool Platin Discs and Hermes Fine Net Discs.

THE PERFECT COMBINATION

To summarize, I would recommend the following as a perfect combination for woodcarving. Start with 100-grit Abranet to remove all of the tool marks and uneven surfaces completely and achieve the final shaping of the form. Then switch to the J-Flex, starting with 150-grit, then 240-grit and finally 400-grit. Finish with a 1,200-grit polishing disc to remove all the minute scratches and produce a perfectly polished surface.

TIP: As with most products, you get what you pay for with abrasives, and the good ones aren't cheap but they do save you a lot of time and energy. It therefore makes sense to pay a little extra for your products and purchase materials that accomplish the job as quickly and efficiently as possible, allowing you to progress onto your next project.

Preparing the carving surface for sanding

Before you begin the sanding process, it is advisable to skim over the sculpture's complete surface with gouges to tidy up any deep gouge cuts and level any uneven areas. It is also important to ensure that details such as eyes, eyelids and awkward corners, are neatly cut and finished without any deep knife marks or messy tool cuts around them. This will create a good base from which to start sanding and, ultimately, make it quicker to complete the job.

GOOD PRACTICE

It is good practice with some subjects, in particular a human figure or animal form, to sand the carving as you work through it. For example, when creating a figure, the methodical approach is to start by forming the head of the subject and working down the body from there. When the details are completed on the head, then the first sanding grit is used to smooth them, bringing them to life and providing a clearer visual understanding of how they will connect to the next area to be worked. This also breaks the sanding task down into smaller chunks, which is of great value when it comes to the final sanding, as you will already have completed the most difficult, lengthiest and important grit.

The surface of the sculpture is being skimmed over to level off any deep gouge cuts or uneven areas before sanding.

The head of this figure has been carved to shape, then sanded with 100-grit to give a clear visual understanding of its balance, detail and life.

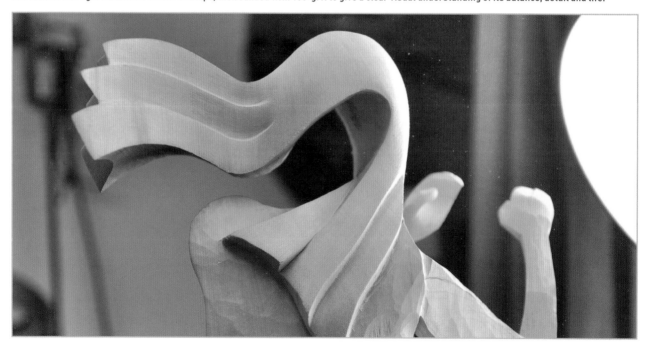

The grit orders

The surface-smoothing procedure by abrasion that we call sanding is accomplished by working progressively from a coarse grit through to a very fine one. There are two routes of sanding grits that I have used successfully for many years:

1 If you are sanding over a large surface that does not have shallow, fine detail, use grits 100, 150, 240, 400 and 1,200 (polishing disc).

2 If you are sanding smaller and more intricate areas, then use grits 120, 180, 240, 400 and 1,200 (polishing disc).

There are exceptions to these routes, which you will learn as you gain experience, and two examples of these are as follows:

- If you are working on very small-scale details, and the depths of these details are fractions of millimeters or inches – an eye, for example – then it is advisable to start the sanding procedure with grits 150, 180 or even 240 in some cases. Otherwise, if you do start with 100 or 120, too much of the surface will quickly be removed, distorting and ruining it.

- If you are carving details of hair in a classical style, then care should be taken not to soften these too much, as the sharp edges and lines are necessary for adding the effect of value (light and shadow) to the finished form. Working through the grits up to 180 should be sufficient depending on the scale.

A close-up of the abrasives with their grit numbers written on them, from the coarsest 100-grit up to the fine 400-grit.

62

The sanding procedure

The most important rule of the sanding procedure is to follow the direction of the grain wherever possible, as sanding across the grain creates deep scratches that are extremely hard to remove.

The first grit that you use, whether 100 or 120, is the most important abrasive, as this has to remove completely every tool mark, blemish and uneven level of depth to finish the natural shaping of the form. This has to be accomplished with meticulous attention to detail, otherwise any marks that are left will persist through the subsequent grades and still show up when the carving is finished and polished. It is perhaps obvious to say, then, that this first grit is the most labor-intensive and time-consuming procedure and uses a lot more material than the other grits (something that should be taken into consideration when you order your abrasives). However, don't try to economize. As soon as the abrasive starts to become less effective and you are having to work much harder and longer to produce the same result, then it is time to throw it away and cut a new piece.

When you reach the stage where you think you have eradicated all of the tool marks from the surface of your wood, then view it in natural light, slowly

Always sand in the direction of the grain.

turning it around to examine the surface as the shadows strike across it. This will show up any undulations and the telltale little dark blemishes left by gouges that haven't been removed.

It is a common misunderstanding to think that gouge marks will come out later on in the sanding procedure after the initial grit, because, quite

The surface of the Swan has been skimmed over to remove all of the deep gouge marks and uneven areas and is ready to be sanded.

The Swan has been sanded through all of the different grits and is ready to be bleached.

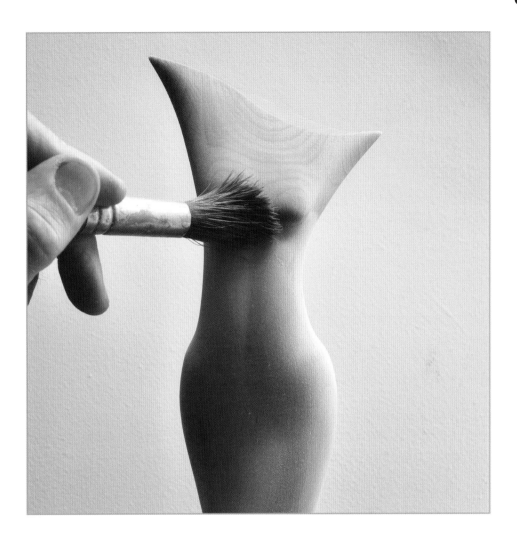

Applying hot water to the sculpture in between each sanding grit raises the fibers in the wood, allowing the subsequent grit to be worked more easily and effectively.

simply, they won't. They may become a lot smoother, but they will persist and ruin the finish. Another common error is to start with a grit that is too fine on a large surface, which, again, will work beautifully at smoothing the gouge marks but won't remove them.

When you have completed the first grit, proceed onto the hot-water technique next.

HOT-WATER TECHNIQUE

The hot-water technique may seem a rather bizarre thing to do to your carving, but it is extremely effective in its objective, as it naturally raises the fibers of the wood, allowing the subsequent grit to be worked more easily and effectively. It also exposes any deeper scratches, gouge marks or areas that may need to be worked a little further before progressing onto the next grit.

Before you apply the hot water, use a soft brush to dust off the carving, paying special attention to any corners, knife cuts or deep folds. Then either pour hot water directly over your carving or paint it over with a clean brush and leave to dry. You can speed up the drying process considerably by using a hair-dryer.

After you have completed the hot-water technique, examine the surface to see if there are any areas that may need to be worked further with the first grit. When you are sure the surface is even, work through each of the subsequent grits up to and including 400, meticulously removing all of the scratches from the previous one and repeating the hot-water process in between every grit. Finally, use the 1,200-grit polishing disc to remove the minute scratches left from the 400 and produce a perfectly polished surface. Your carving is now ready for you to apply the finish of your choice.

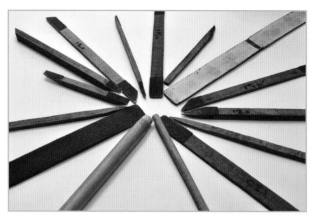

Bespoke sanding sticks can be made and shaped for working into any awkward areas of the carving.

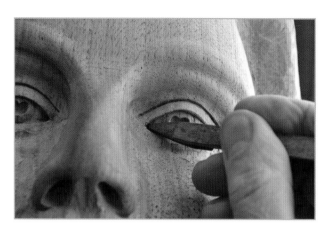

A pointed sanding stick is vital to shape and smooth the inner corner of details such as eyes.

Sanding tips and tricks

Sanding sticks are an excellent solution to many awkward and inaccessible areas. These can be cut to size from any little offcuts of wood with their ends shaped to the correct angle, contour or size required for the application. The ends of the sticks are then placed carefully on the abrasive and their shape transferred onto it with a sharpened pencil. The sandpaper is cut to this size and stuck on the stick with a spot of instant glue. Once worn, it can easily be removed with a knife, after which the end of the stick is given a quick rub over with 100-grit, and is ready to be used again. For many applications, the abrasive can easily be held in place on the stick without the need to glue it in position.

Similar to sanding sticks, emery manicure boards are also useful for reaching into awkward areas and are available in many different grits. They are easily trimmed to the required shape and can be cut back when worn.

Left and bottom left: Abrasives can be held in position on appropriately shaped sticks to work on areas of detail.

Below: Emery boards can be trimmed to shape and used to reach awkward areas of detail.

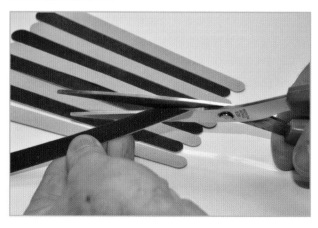

Right: Diamond rotary burrs are an effective tool for smoothing small hollowed areas by hand.

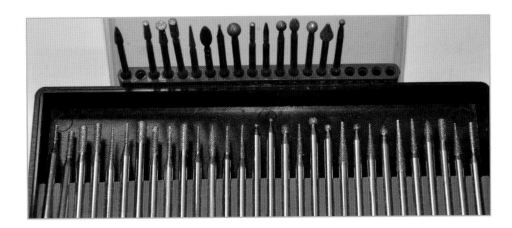

Below: A ¹⁄₃₂in (1mm) diamond sphere is used to delicately shape the Polar Bear's nostrils.

A ⅛in (3mm) diamond sphere is used to smooth the pupil of an eye.

Diamond rotary burrs are made for power-carving tools and have a very fine composition of diamond-impregnated particles on their formed working edge. These are used as a finishing tool for various applications but can also be used to great effect by hand to smooth the surface of hollowed areas, such as the pupil of an eye, nostrils and ears. They can be bought cheaply in sets such as the ones pictured above and are available in many different shapes and sizes for a multitude of applications.

Obviously, there are many ways in which you can roll or fold sandpaper to shape it to the appropriate angle for the area you are working on. However, the method shown on the right is particularly effective, as it forms a very rigid spine from the tip to the end, allowing you to apply a fair amount of pressure to the detail you are sanding. You can also slide a sanding stick into the end to give you even more rigidity and dexterity of use.

If you follow these simple guidelines with patience, perseverance and meticulous attention to detail, then you will always be able to bring your projects to life with a perfectly polished finish.

DESIGN

DESIGN AND PROJECT PLANNING ARE THE FOUNDATIONAL, CREATIVE AND TECHNICAL SKILLS THAT WE MUST ALL EMBRACE EACH TIME WE EMBARK ON A NEW PROJECT IN ORDER TO DEVELOP OUR IDEAS AND TRANSFORM OUR CONCEPT OR VISION INTO A THREE-DIMENSIONAL FORM. IT IS THE MOST IMPORTANT MOMENT, WHEN WE USE OUR IMAGINATIONS TO EXPLORE AND STRETCH OUR CONCEPTS IN COUNTLESS DIRECTIONS.

This chapter is an introduction to the subject of design and the essential elements and principles upon which successful design is founded. All these should be carefully considered and practiced when creating your forms. Your original idea is first designed and developed on paper to organize visually all of the elements of its composition and balance their relationship with one another. Alongside the design, you must also carefully consider the problems that may arise when creating the form in the medium and what procedures or solutions will be necessary to overcome them to ensure that the design is viable. When all the elements of the design are eventually balanced, and you have considered every detail of its completion, then you can begin transforming it into the wood.

The design and development principles of three-dimensional work constitute a profound, fascinating and extremely rewarding subject that is as important to learn about as the technical production of the work. Creativity and technique are dependent on one another for success, as one cannot function effectively without the other. Therefore, a balance of study and practice should be divided between these two areas to make sure of a successful outcome. The truth is, if you don't attempt your own designs then you will be stuck with the uninspiring choice of copying the plans of other people, which will slow your progress, stifle your creativity and, ultimately, frustrate and discourage you. Conversely, if you are an independent learner, embrace the designing as well as the production, then you will be totally free to explore your creative ideas in whatever subject, style or form that you choose.

'Rehana' by Andrew Thomas. Bronze on granite.

Form is the external appearance of the shape and structure of an object; the organized composition of the visual components in a united wholeness.

Concept is the birth of an idea, either through your inner creativity or by observation of a subject that you wish to study and represent. It is either a single form or composition of forms, representing reality, partially abstracted reality or a fully abstracted form. Generally speaking, the concept should symbolize or express a message or meaning, intended to create an impact on, or challenge to, the viewer's senses.

Elements of design

The elements of design are the individual components or fundamental building blocks that are used in relationship with the principles of design to create an organized, balanced form that ultimately establishes the unification or harmony of a form's composition. Not every sculpture has all of the elements within its design, but a few of them at least should be employed. These individual elements are as follows:

POSITIVE SPACE

Positive space (see top right) is the area that is filled by the object's volume or mass. It is used in relationship with negative space to balance the composition of the design.

NEGATIVE SPACE

Negative space (see right) is the area immediately around the positive mass of the sculpture, which can be used to enhance its profile edges and to bring balance to an asymmetrical form. It can also be used to create an interesting or artistically relevant shape in relation to the spatial position and form of the positive mass.

The top picture represents the positive space or composition of the volumes of a sculpture, whereas the dark areas in the picture below represent the negative space, which can be used effectively in relationship to the positive space to enhance its profile edges.

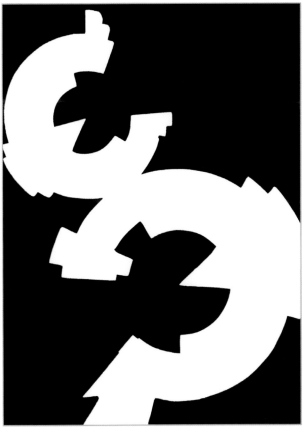

PLANE

Plane refers to the flat or level surface areas
of a sculpture and their spatial direction.

SHAPE

Shape is the entirety of the sculptured form.

VALUE

Value is how the light and shadow strike across the
contours, undulations, textures, planes and other
detailed areas of the form (see the example on
the right and at the top right of page 71). The use
of value is far more effective on a lighter-colored
wood, as the dark shadows are more visible against
the light surfaces and contours of the medium.
It can be used very effectively to enhance the life
of a sculpture and the impact of its detail.

TEXTURE

Texture is the tactile quality of the surface, which
can be finished in a multitude of ways, to create
the effects that enhance the experience of the
sculpture. The urge to smooth one's hands over
the surface of a form can be very hard to resist,
and this is an important part of the appreciation
of sculpture and should be encouraged. Physical
contact with the medium somehow connects the
viewer to the form in a deeper way, effectuating
a heightened experience of the senses, and the
texture is vital to this experience.

COLOR

Color is the natural appearance of the medium,
which in this instance is wood, of which there are
many different colors and species. When planning a
project, consideration should always be given to the
selection of an appropriate species of wood
and the type of finish that will be used for the subject,
as this will affect the final color and therefore the

The use of value works particularly well on lighter-colored woods, dramatically enhancing the life of the sculpture.

experience of the viewer. So, for example, if you are
carving a white swan, then to use a piece of lime
finished with wood bleach would be an appropriate
color choice.

MASS

Mass is the main body of the medium that we
are using to make our sculpture – in this case,
wood. The mass of a sculpture may be made up
of a number of volumes joined together to form
a complex structure.

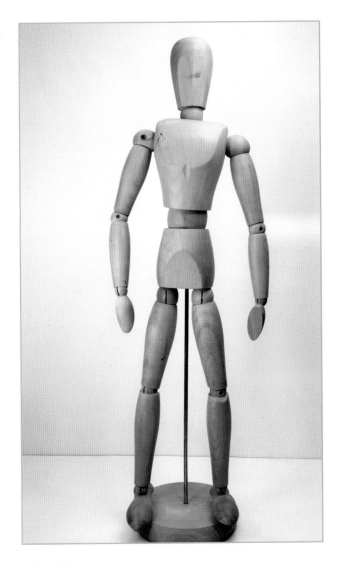

VOLUME

In sculpture, volume is a structured or shaped quantity of mass, which has definite form in all three dimensions. The mass of a piece of sculpture may be either a single volume or made up of a number of volumes. For example, a bunch of grapes consists of one volume for each individual grape, but, although each volume is joined to other volumes, it is identified as a separate unit that is organized in a spatial arrangement of many volumes. If this bunch of grapes were to be placed into a container or bag, then all the individual volumes would become just one volume.

The artist's mannequin doll, seen above, is a good example of how many volumes are connected together to form a mass that we recognize as a human figure. If we were studying the naked human figure with the aim of reproducing it in our chosen medium, then we must examine each of the volumes individually to help us to understand how the underlying life structures of the form (the complex anatomical layering of muscle and tendons on bones) are organized in each of the volumes and how each volume relates to its adjoining one. If the mannequin or human figure were clothed, then the number of volumes would be significantly reduced. The clothed volumes would then have different complexities because of the underlying life structures and they would need to be studied closely to understand how the volumes within them behave in relation to the material on their surface – for example, how the folds of the clothes radiate from such areas as the shoulders, elbows, hips and knees.

Principles of design

The principles of design can be thought of as the application of the elements – what we do with them, how we arrange, construct or bring order to them. Many artists have the natural ability to use these principles intuitively, which is often called 'having a good eye' for composition, detail and balance of form. The individual principles are as follows:

BALANCE

The balance of a three-dimensional design can perhaps be summarized simply as a form that sits comfortably on the eye. However, to produce this balance requires a considerable degree of observation, contemplation and perception by the artist to enable them to come up with a design where all of the volumes not only work in harmony with each other but also with the negative space that is part of the sculpture.

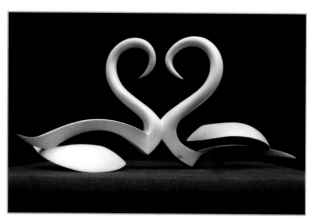

Positive and negative space have been used in harmony together to produce an asymmetrical design that sits comfortably on the eye.

Creating movement in your sculpture can dramatically enhance its life and the visual impact of the subject.

Asymmetrical balance can be used effectively and creatively, giving the artist more freedom with the design to create harmonious relationships between the negative and positive spaces, bringing life to the negative space and harmony within the overall composition of the sculpture (see example above).

A square angle has been used within this elliptical sculpture to create contrast in its composition, naturally drawing the eye into the main large piercing.

PROPORTION

Proportion is the scale of the form and the relationship between its details and its various volumes, meaning that each of the individual parts of the sculpture should be formed and balanced in relation to one another. For example, if you are designing a figurative composition depicting an adult and child, then you will need to calculate accurately the scale of each individual figure to ensure that their proportions are harmonious.

MOVEMENT

Movement in sculpture is about portraying convincingly the directional energy of the form in relation to action, gravity and motion. If used effectively, it can profoundly intensify the life and dynamic vitality of the form, dramatically enhancing the impact of its visual energy (see example top right).

CONTRAST

Contrast in a sculpture can create a more striking relationship between the various elements of the design and be used to draw the eye towards different areas of the form. This can be employed in many creative ways, for example, by creating a change of directional movement between two volumes, by merging smooth and rough textures together or by using space and mass in a balanced relationship with one another (see example on left).

The picture on the left demonstrates the use of rhythm or repetition in a sculpture, which was designed to create the feeling of sound waves. The picture on the right embodies all of the elements and principles of design in its composition, creating a unified and harmonious form.

It is important to establish the correct balance of contrast so that the elements work in harmony with one another and do not cause confusion in the composition.

EMPHASIS

Not to be confused with contrast, emphasis is achieved by using one or more of the design elements to create a dominant focal point or powerful visual impact within the composition of the form. This can be achieved by, for example: a dramatic change of size between volumes; using value to bring deep shadow into a hollow space of the form; using color variations; or applying other media, such as metal, to enhance and strengthen areas of the composition. The use of emphasis should always be carefully considered in relationship with the other elements of the composition, to work with them to bring balance and unity to the composition.

RHYTHM AND REPETITION

Rhythm can be structured effectively within the design of a sculpture by repeating one or more of its elements to create a harmonious sequence or pattern using either regular or irregular forms in a balanced composition (see example top left).

HARMONY AND UNITY

Harmony is the end result of the sculpture after all of the design elements and principles are sensitively applied and are working gloriously together to create a wholeness or fusion in the complete composition of the form (see example top right).

GOLDEN RULE It doesn't have to be complex to be a good design – in fact, quite the opposite is often true. When you feel that your design is successfully delivering the essence of your concept and that all of the elements are in harmony with one another, then you have succeeded.

Real-life studies are of the utmost importance to practice but are intensive and should be balanced with creating freedom of expression (abstract) sculptures.

Art styles

There are evidently a multitude of artistic styles from many different periods that you can study and practice and in which you can create forms. But, for the purposes of this book we shall only be focusing on three: realism, stylized (part-representational/part-abstract) and abstract.

REALISM: TECHNICAL STUDIES

Technical projects are those that require the close study of a realistic subject to be replicated in a chosen medium, as near to the real-life form as possible. The subject can be an animate form, such as the human figure, or an inanimate object, like folds of fabric for instance. Intensive studies are made of the real-life subject, a live model or an object being the most useful if available, which will provide a clear three-dimensional visual reference that can be examined closely to identify the surface structure and its anatomy or detail. The subject can then be meticulously and methodically copied onto the surface of the medium, utilizing multiple tool techniques and several different measuring instruments and methods.

Some of the measuring instruments and methods used for realism studies, pictured on the facing page are, from left to right:

- Calipers – used for measuring the internal and external diameters and thicknesses of the subject.

- Profile gauges – used for taking a profile reading from a form. The gauge is gently pressed onto the subject and takes the exact profile pattern, which can then be used as a reference to transfer the contour onto the medium. These are available in a variety of different sizes and materials.

- Vernier calipers – three instruments in one, which are used for measuring thicknesses, internal and external diameters and depths. This is an extremely useful instrument that should be your first choice of measuring tool.

- Rules – you will need a 6in (15cm) and a 12in (30cm) one for different applications. The blue one pictured is flexible and unbreakable so it can be used to measure and mark around contours.

Real-life studies can be, and usually are, quite intense projects, as the woodcarver has very little freedom to exercise creativity on the form. They are about observation, problem solving, measuring and tool techniques, all of which are of the utmost importance to learn, and with enough practice over time will make a huge contribution towards our mastering of the medium.

STYLIZATION

Stylized form falls comfortably in between realism and abstract form so it could be described as a simplification of realism, a part-representational or part-abstracted form. The overall composition is representational, but the strict rules of realism are relaxed, thus allowing artists far more creative freedom to express their ideas and interpretation of the subject detail. The Cat project on page 110 is a good example of this style, as the realism of

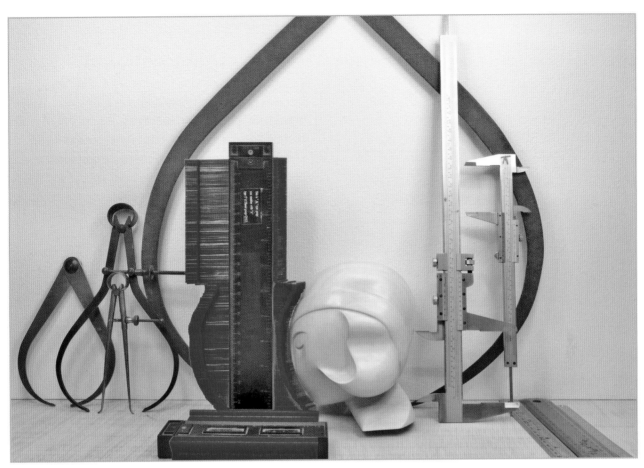

These are some of the instruments that are used for measuring and taking profiles from real-life studies.

the facial details, legs, feet and tail are all partially abstracted to simplify the subject for the beginner. The finished form, however, still convincingly represents what we all recognize as a cat, having just enough detail to produce a contemporary, elegant feline form.

ABSTRACT – FREEDOM OF EXPRESSION

Abstract art, or freedom of expression, is the opposite of a realistic technical study, as it does not endeavor to represent reality as we see it but instead delineates a visual expression of form in a part- or non-representational arrangement. This requires artists to use their creativity, to contemplate the substance of their subject or concept and express this essence harmoniously into the composition of their design and form. For example, the picture on the right shows a sculpture that represents the incredible power of the sea and the wind. The elements of the positive and negative

space are balanced with one another, and the principle of movement is harnessed in relation to gravity to create a dynamic energy within the form.

Learning to design form in an abstract style is vital to the essential development of our inner creativity and should be practiced equally alongside real-life studies.

Negative space draws the eye into the heart of this representational sculpture, thereby enhancing the effect of the positive space.

The picture above is of a more representational form, designed to convey the classical heritage of the instrument combined with the fluid essence of its tonal waves. Negative space has been used to draw the eye into the heart of the form, which dramatically enhances the effect of the positive space and powerfully distributes its flow of energy down through the form.

GOLDEN RULE Always try to be experimental with your designs. Look for new challenges, and don't be afraid to take risks. The more you diversify from subject to subject, be it representational or abstract, the more you will learn and understand about the complexities of form in three dimensions.

A successfully designed sculpture should impact on viewers' senses and challenge them to consider its meaning, which will naturally engage them with the form as they absorb its essence, resulting in a deeper experience and a greater appreciation of its entity. Thus it is important to encourage this interaction by not making this too easy – a sense of mystery is a positive attribute.

Sketching

Sketching is an essential skill in transferring ideas from the imagination into a tangible form on paper. They can then be analysed, further developed and brought to order using the elements and principles of design to balance the composition. This is clearly a crucial part of the project-planning process, which will provide you with a visual understanding of the form and what problems may occur when you try to realize it. This should always be approached with a positive mindset, as you do not need to have a degree in fine art to produce small, simple design sketches, but some effort must be made because they are vital in order for you to produce your own original work.

A recommended approach to this is to make a series of different sketches all next to one another, taking each detail that works effectively on the eye and then further developing it in the subsequent sketch. You can then use each sketch as a visual reference to make the subtle changes necessary to arrive at the correct balance and composition of the design. If, on the other hand, you were to make only one drawing and continuously erase the pencil lines then it would be counter-productive, as the visual references of the development journey would be lost and confusion created.

On the facing page is a simple example showing the development of a female figure through six sketches. The first four show the development of the design and the last two, the subtle balancing of the contour lines. The picture (image 7) shows the finished sculpture of the female figure in the sketches.

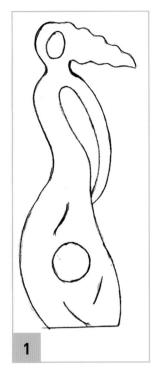

1

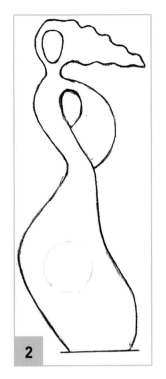

2

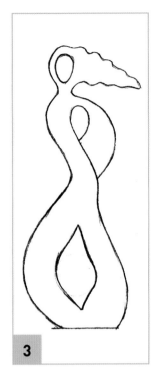

3

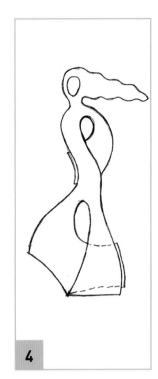

4

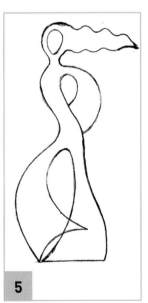

5

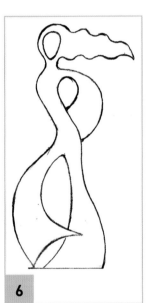

6

A final thought

Learning about the elements and principles of design and applying them creatively to your ideas and concepts will profoundly enrich your understanding of form and significantly aid the development of your progress. Consequently, this will enhance your appreciation of art considerably, as you will have a much deeper awareness of what you are viewing and what the artist has tried to achieve with their work.

7

SCALE DRAWINGS

THE QUICKEST AND MOST EFFECTIVE METHOD TO BEGIN WORK ON THE ACTUAL FORM OF YOUR DESIGN IS TO PREPARE TWO SCALE DRAWINGS, ONE OF ITS FRONT PROFILE AND ONE OF THE SIDE. THESE DRAWINGS ARE THEN TRANSFERRED ONTO YOUR WOOD IN PERFECT ALIGNMENT WITH EACH OTHER, AND THE WASTE WOOD IS CUT AWAY, LEAVING YOU WITH THE OUTLINE OF YOUR DESIGN IN POSITION READY TO START SHAPING IT AND DEVELOPING THE DETAIL.

It is of the utmost importance that these profile drawings are in perfect scale and alignment with each other before the block is cut, otherwise the result could end up at best distorted and may have to be completely scrapped.

1 Here is an example showing the front and side profiles of the Emperor Penguin project (see page 148) that are in scale and alignment with one another. All of the dimensions and details from one profile have been squared across to the other to check for perfect alignment before cutting.

2 Here is another example of the Emperor Penguin, but these profiles are not in scale or alignment with one another. If they were to be applied to the wood and cut out, the two profiles would not meet properly and consequently the job would have to be scrapped and started again.

Scale

When you have accurately produced your scale drawings, the next step is to enlarge them to the correct scale for your wood. This will normally be determined by the depth or thickness of your wood, as this is usually the limiting factor for the scale of the carving. For instance, if the maximum depth of your wood is 4in (100mm), then the appropriate design profile to be placed on this edge of the wood is enlarged to this size with the use of a scanner or photocopier. When this has been accomplished, you can then measure the exact height of this enlarged profile and apply this dimension to the other scale profile when it is scanned or copied. The two profiles should then be at the exact scale for your wood and in perfect scale with one another. They can finally be printed out onto card, cut out to use as templates and also as references from which to measure.

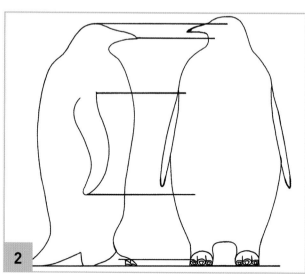

1

2

Abstract designs

It is not always possible to visualize and prepare both profiles of the design, especially when you are designing abstract forms. The concept is developed on paper to balance, problem solve and understand the variables on at least one side or view of the form. But on many occasions you may need to feel your way in and develop and balance the three-dimensional aspects of the form as it evolves. If this is the case, then it is perfectly acceptable to apply this one-profile design onto the appropriate side of your wood, cut it out and then start your work from there. However, it is also essential that you allow yourself enough depth in the wood to ensure that the scale and proportions of the design are in balance with each other from all angles in three dimension (for more on this, see the Design chapter starting on page 66).

To simplify the procedure of calculating the scale or size of the profile drawings that are supplied in this book, a borderline has been marked at the outer limit on each of the four sides. When you are enlarging the drawings, these lines can be used as a reference between which to measure, to verify that the front and side profiles are in scale with one another, and that the scale is correct for the size of your wood.

Borderlines have been added to the profile drawings as a helpful reference when measuring size or scale.

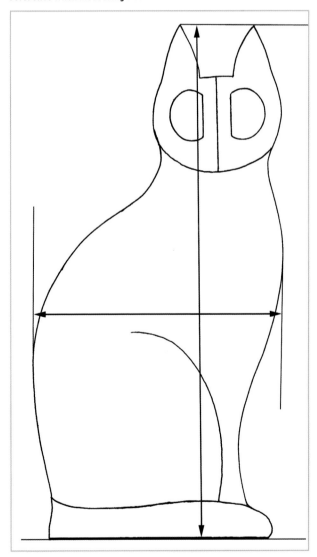

CUTTING PROFILES

THE CUTTING OF THE SUBJECT'S PROFILES IS THE PROCEDURE OF REMOVING ALL OF THE WASTE WOOD FROM THE PROFILE EDGE OF THE DESIGN THAT YOU ARE CARVING, ALLOWING YOU TO START THE CARVING PROCESS ACCURATELY FROM THIS PRECISE OUTER LINE OF THE SUBJECT. IT IS BENEFICIAL TO DO THIS AS EFFICIENTLY AS POSSIBLE, SO THAT YOU CAN QUICKLY PROGRESS TO EXECUTING THE CARVING.

Cutting your wood

There are two ways to cut the profiles of your designs: either with a bandsaw or by hand.

BANDSAWING

The quickest and most effective way to cut your two profiles is with a bandsaw fitted with a very sharp ¼in (6mm), four-teeth-per-inch (4tpi – tpi is the international standard system), skip-toothed blade. If you do not have your own bandsaw, then it shouldn't be too difficult to find someone who has – a local woodturner, carver or cabinet-maker should be able to help.

Before you apply the designs to your block of wood, you must first ensure that the block is planed perfectly flat and square on the two sides that will be in contact with the bandsaw table (the opposite sides to those on which you will draw your design), so that the front and side profiles line up precisely with one another when cut.

1   To transfer your designs onto the wood, use the cardboard templates onto which you printed your designs, as described on page 76, and draw the front profile onto your block first. Use a square to transfer the level of the front profile around to the side of the wood, then draw the side view onto the side of your block at this precise level. It is also good practice to square around details such as the tip of the beak of a bird, the fingertips on a hand or any other point of reference to ensure that these details are accurately in line and scale from both profiles.

Safety first

- Always use a sharp blade
- Always fit a dust collector
- Always wear eye protection
- Always wear a dust mask

1

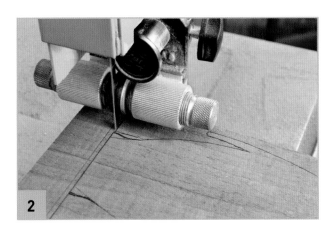

Be very careful to ensure that both profiles are facing in the right direction, otherwise your bandsawn block will be back to front.

2   You will need to leave a square section at the base of your block, which will be used for securing it to your carving vise. The width will obviously vary depending on your design, but the depth should be approximately 1½in (40mm) thick so that, if necessary, you can use substantial-sized screws to secure the block to your vise.

3   The first profile to be cut is determined by the simplest side of the design. If possible, this should be cut in one or two continuous pieces. This is important because the block has to be re-formed square again for the second profile cut, which would be impossible otherwise. For example, if you were cutting out a bust, then you would start with the front view profile because this can generally be cut in one piece. If you were to start with the side view, then by the time you had cut around the nose, mouth and chin areas, you would have many pieces to try to reconstruct back into a square block, which would be difficult. So, starting with the simplest profile, cut directly along the very outer edge of the line, all of the way around its contour, ending at the square base.

4   You then need to re-form the wood back into its original square block to complete the cutting of the side profile. Do this carefully, using good-quality masking tape and making sure that you do not tape onto the back edge of the block that will be in contact with the bandsaw bed, as this will mean the block – and consequently your cut – will not be level.

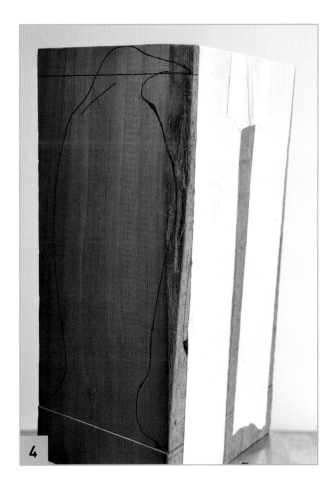

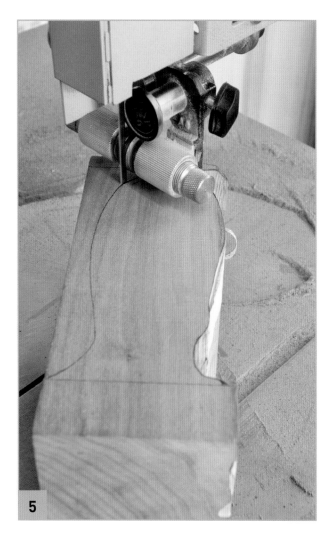

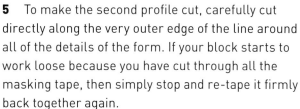

5

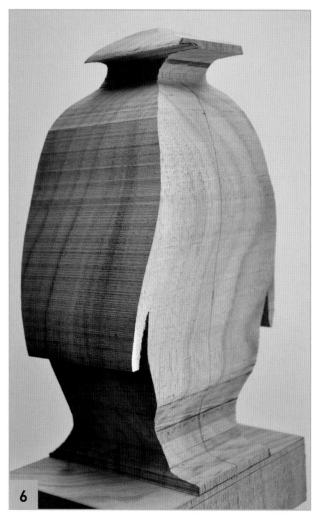

6

5   To make the second profile cut, carefully cut directly along the very outer edge of the line around all of the details of the form. If your block starts to work loose because you have cut through all the masking tape, then simply stop and re-tape it firmly back together again.

6   Both profiles have been cut and your piece is ready to be secured to the vise.

If you do not have access to a bandsaw then, depending on the depth of your wood, you may be able to use either a coping saw or a fret saw to cut one, or maybe even both, of your design profiles.

TIP Quite often while bandsawing design profiles, the need arises to back the blade out of a cut. This procedure has to be accomplished very carefully, by cutting into the wood ½–1in (13–25mm) at a time and then backing the blade out again to clear the channel of the fine dust that builds up very quickly directly behind the blade. If this is not done, then you run the risk of getting the blade stuck in its own channel, which can be very difficult to rectify. If this does happen at any point, do not force the blade forwards or you will pull it off the wheels of the bandsaw. You should stop the machine and try to unblock the channel using a very thin rule or something similar that is small enough to poke and scratch the channel clear again. If all else fails, then you will need to cut the blade and fit a new one.

CUTTING PROFILES BY HAND

Preparing your block for carving by hand requires the complete opposite to the bandsawing method, as you will only be able to follow one profile from the square edge accurately. So, as a rule, the first profile to be cut should always be the more complex one.

1 Transfer the profile drawing onto the planed block using the same method as described for bandsawing and leaving a square section at its base, then draw straight lines around this profile, at a minimum of ⅛in (2–3mm) away from the profile line.

2 Secure your block to your woodcarving vise and use a sharp panel saw to remove the waste wood along the straight lines.

3 Use a selection of gouges of the correct curvature to pare the wood accurately and squarely back to the profile line.

4 Use a square to help ensure the profile is cut level across the wood.

5 The second profile line is slightly more difficult to apply to the block, as you will not have a straight edge onto which to draw it, so you will need to use a combination of sighting and measuring to ensure that it is accurately in place.

- Hold the template in position on the wood but do not distort its dimensions by bending it around the curvature of the first profile cut.

- Start your line at the point where the template is touching the wood.

- Continue the line by looking past the template to the block behind (sighting) and drawing it in position on your block.

- Use your template as a reference to measure from and check for its accuracy on the block, making any necessary adjustments.

6 Repeat steps 1–4 above, cutting neatly back to this second profile line, completing this procedure by hand and leaving the subject ready to be carved.

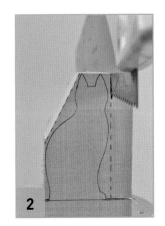

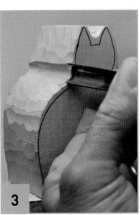

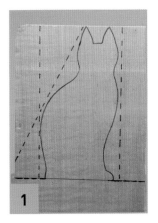

GRAIN DIRECTION

Difficulty level: 1/10
on the beginner's scale

Time to complete:
approximately 1 hour

UNDERSTANDING THE COMPLEXITIES OF WOOD GRAIN AND HOW TO CARVE IT EFFECTIVELY CAN BE A LITTLE CONFUSING TO THE BEGINNER. THIS SIMPLE EXERCISE SHOULD HELP, AS IT WILL GIVE YOU SOME PRACTICAL EXPERIENCE AND KNOWLEDGE OF HOW TO APPROACH THE DIFFERENT GRAIN DIRECTIONS.

End grain

If you were to make a horizontal cut across a tree trunk and look at the annual growth rings, then you would be looking at the end grain. So, the end grain of your block or plank of wood will be at the top and bottom between the vertical wood grain stripes. End grain is much harder to carve because of the fiber endings, so some consideration should always be given to its direction when planning your project. If, for instance, the dimensions of your project are of a portrait proportion, then the grain should be running vertically up through the form; if your subject is landscape, then it should run horizontally.

Another consideration is to ensure that you use the supreme strength of the grain running vertically through any vulnerable areas of detail whenever possible, as the horizontal stripes of the grain are much weaker and far more prone to snapping when pressure is applied to them around fine detail.

End grain

End grain

End grain

TOOLS

No. 2/20
No. 7/14

WOOD

Lime (basswood)

Dimensions before
cutting profile:
H 8 x W 3½ x D 1½in
(200 x 90 x 40mm)

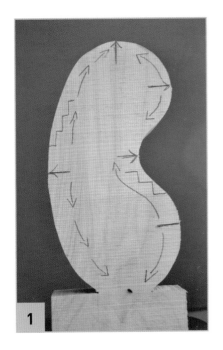

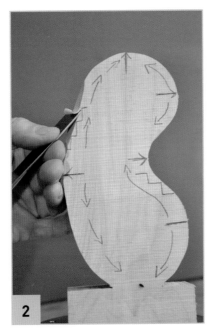

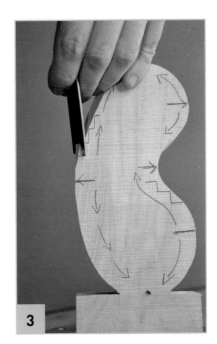

The exercise

The objective is to create a
gentle curved edge over the
entire surface of the form as
in picture 11 on page 85.

1 Transfer the design supplied
onto a piece of lime wood
with the grain running vertically
through the design. Now cut it
out and mount it securely on
your vise. The design has the
carving directions marked
onto the wood for you to follow.
Mark all of these arrows onto
your wood and also draw the
little steps on the left and right.

2 Carve with the grain, meaning
cut in the direction that the
wood fibers are flowing, working
down over the steps that you have
drawn and creating a gentle curve
over this edge. This is the correct
approach to the grain, as there
is nothing here that will cause
any resistance to the gouge as it
moves in this direction. Use your
No. 2/20 to do this, and feel how
easily it slices through the grain.

3 The horizontal arrows that
are marked on both sides
of the wood show the exact
positions where you need to
change cutting direction; if
you do not change direction at
these points, you will be cutting
against the grain. This will result
in the blade naturally trying to
follow the line of the grain, which
will eventually break out if you
persist with the cut. In order
to change direction, you need to
start your cut just past the peak
of the curved profile so that the
grain will not lift. Experiment with
cutting against the grain before
the peak of the curve, feel the
resistance in the cut and observe
how your gouge naturally wants
to follow the stripe of the grain.
Break it out if you wish – it's only
a test piece of wood, and it is a
good exercise to learn how it
behaves in this situation.

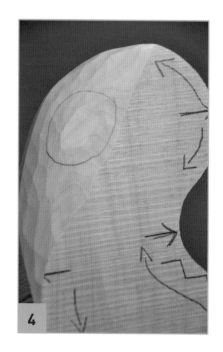

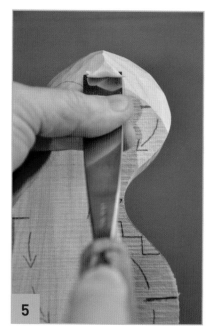

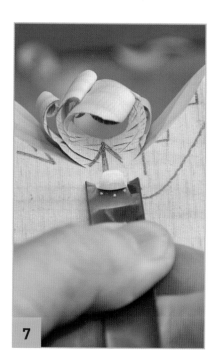

4 Another way of testing to see if you are working against the grain is to look at the texture and color of your gouge cuts. When you are following the grain correctly, you will notice that each gouge cut is smooth, shiny and the same color as the wood. On the other hand, if you have cut against the grain then the cut will have a rough, matt texture and be lighter in color. When you have rounded this end over a little more, make a small cut in the wrong direction to see how this appears and feels.

You can now work on the right side of the wood, following the direction of the arrows and repeating the process to curve this edge as you did on the left side.

5 You should now have both the left and right upper sides curved over from the edge and meeting in the middle at the top of the wood. Next, simply follow the grain in the direction of the arrow, up and over the end grain at the top, paring the wood away until it is even with both left and right edges.

6 Working on the right-hand side of the form now, you come to the area where the contour of the edge sweeps in towards the center of the wood. This area requires you to follow the grain by cutting inwards into the curve from both directions.

7 As you can see in the picture, the wood in the center of the curve will not naturally chip out and will need to be removed by cutting across the grain. Do this with your No. 7/14, which is far

more curved than the No. 2 that you have been using so far for the sides of the form and is therefore more appropriate for the tighter curvature of this area of the design.

8

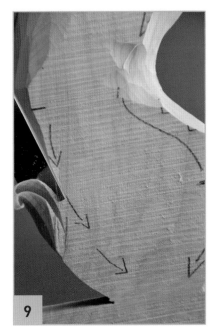

9

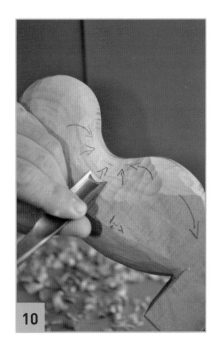

10

8 Cuts being made across the grain at right angles are simple to do, as you are neither carving with nor against the grain. Start your cut a short way back from the center and work into the tight curve to remove the lifted wood on both sides as cleanly and evenly as you can. You can then carve horizontally across the opposite edge on the left side, but using the No. 2/20 again to curve it over in the position between the grain directions where the left horizontal arrow is drawn on the wood.

9 Now shape the lower edges on both sides of the form, following the grain in the correct direction.

10 The complete surface can now be contoured and blended into the curved edges. Notice how the grain is flowing around the inner contour, almost guiding you in the direction of cut.

11 The wood has now been shaped evenly over the complete surface of this side, and the exercise is complete. But why not carve the other side as well and experiment by changing the outer profile to make your own first original design? This will give you some more valuable experience of how to approach the grain before you start the more complex projects in this book.

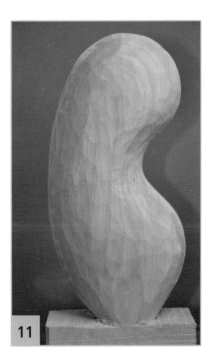

11

Sanding

When you have completed this exercise, you can use it as a piece on which to experiment by practising sanding the form through all of the grits, using the hot-water technique in between each one, following the techniques and methods outlined on pages 62–63.

THE PROJECTS

The following projects have been
designed as a progressive course
for you to work through, each in turn
building on the advancement of your
technical and creative skills. You will
find that each design is adaptable,
enabling you to develop it further
by adding your own artistic ideas and
fingerprint. It is recommended that you
do this, as it will help you to progress
from following the instructions in this
book through to producing your own
original works of art.

WAVE

Difficulty level: 2/10 on the beginner's scale

Time to complete: 10–15 hours

WAVE IS A VERY SIMPLE FORM FOR THE BEGINNER TO CARVE, AND ONE THAT IS FUN TO WORK THROUGH AND EXTREMELY REWARDING TO CREATE. IT IS A REPRESENTATION OF A WAVE, DEPICTING ITS MOTION IN RELATION TO GRAVITY, ENHANCED BY THE NEGATIVE SPACE IN THE HOLLOW CENTER.

This design is simplicity itself, as it is purely a circle within a circle but with gentle flowing lines on the edges. It will help you to understand how to approach the grain in these areas, working the contour of the mass evenly to great effect. It is also a subtle introduction to design, as the whole piece can easily be modified to accommodate your own ideas – something that is highly recommended.

There are many ways in which you can adapt this design. The first and most obvious is to alter the position or size of the inner circle, which will naturally give a different balance to the sculpture. Another option is to dispense with the separation, keeping the form solid but completely rounding over the edges. The flat square edges at the separation could also be curved so that they flow from the sides of the sculpture around to the outer edges, blending into a point rather than the square end. These are just a few ideas. Try to get your own creative juices flowing and develop and explore an original variation of the concept.

TOOLS

No. 3/30
No. 7/20

WOOD

Lime (basswood)

Dimensions before cutting profile: H 9 x W 11 x D 4½in (229 x 280 x 114mm)

Dimensions of Wave: H 8½ x W 8½ x D 4⅜in (216 x 216 x 111mm)

Lime wood is very soft to carve and great for a first project, as it is quite forgiving if you carve it against the grain. The scale of your sculpture will depend on the size of wood that you purchase, but the height/width of the block should be approximately twice that of the depth. You must also allow at least 1½in (40mm) on the base for you to attach it to your vise.

What you will learn

- How to cut a design from one profile view
- How to create a piercing through the sculpture
- The benefits of a flexible rule
- How to approach the grain and create a curved contour
- How to protect vulnerable areas of the sculpture
- The benefits of skimming the surface before sanding
- How to polish the sculpture using waxes
- How to make an appropriate base
- The effect of boiled linseed oil on walnut

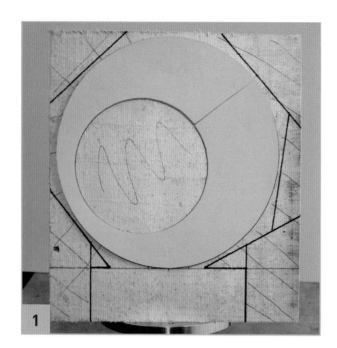

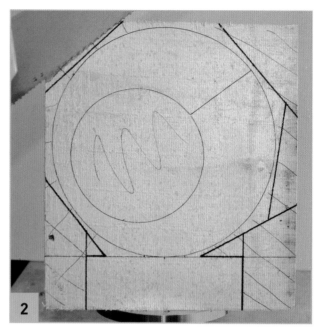

SCALE DESIGN AND CUTTING OUT

Please note, the direction of the grain for this project should be running vertically up through your design.

Measure the depth/thickness of your wood and double this dimension to calculate the correct size for your design.

Add 1½in (40mm) extra at the base of the circle for fixing to your vise. Use either a scanner or photocopier to enlarge the design to your required size. Print this onto a piece of card and cut it out very carefully following the line. Picture 1 above shows this complete.

Scale design

By hand

1 Carefully hold the design template in position on your wood and draw around it using a fine-tipped ink marker. Now draw a square base at the bottom of the circle big enough to secure it onto your faceplate. Repeat these steps on the opposite side of your wood. Draw a series of straight lines around the circle and base at a distance of approximately ⅛in (3mm) from the design. These lines will be used as a cutting guide to remove the excess wood.

2 Carefully secure your block in a vise or with a clamp and use a panel saw to cut along the marked straight lines to remove the excess wood. Now cut along the straight line on the right of the design that joins the outer circle with the inner one.

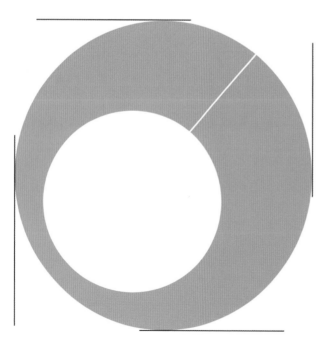

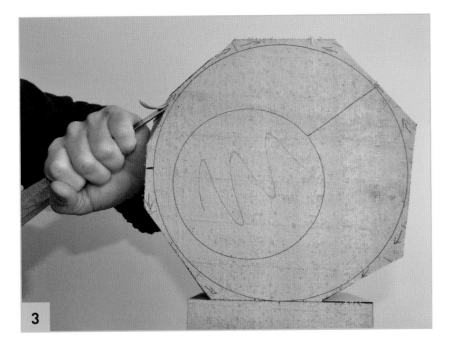

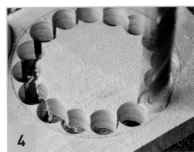

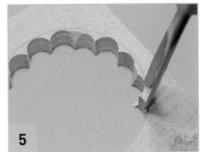

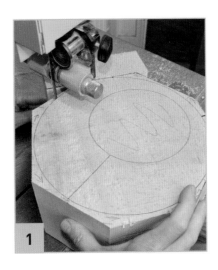

3 Secure your block safely to your carving vise. Hold the No. 3/30 correctly, as shown, and pare the wood back to the line of the circle, cutting with the grain in the direction of the marked arrows.

TIP Use a try square to ensure that your cuts are level across the edge of the wood.

4 To remove the wood from the inner circle, use a large brad-point drill bit to make a series of adjoining drill holes around the inner line of the circle until your drill holes meet up and the center pops out.

5 Use the No. 7/20 to pare the wood back carefully to the line. Work from both outer edges evenly in towards the center of the hole.

Using a bandsaw

1 Cut along the top edge of the square base, at the bottom of the circle and inwards from both directions, until you reach approximately ¾in (20mm) from the center on each side. Don't forget to keep backing your blade out every ½–1in (13–25mm) so as to keep the channel behind the blade clear of fine dust and eliminate the risk of it becoming stuck (see Tip on page 80).

Now cut directly along the outer edge of the line, all of the way around the outer circle and along the straight line on the right of the design that joins the outer circle with the inner one. Lastly, cut around the inner circle.

2 You can now mount your bandsawn block securely on your vise ready for carving.

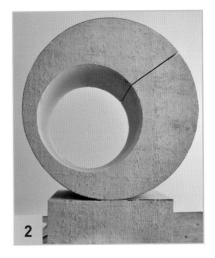

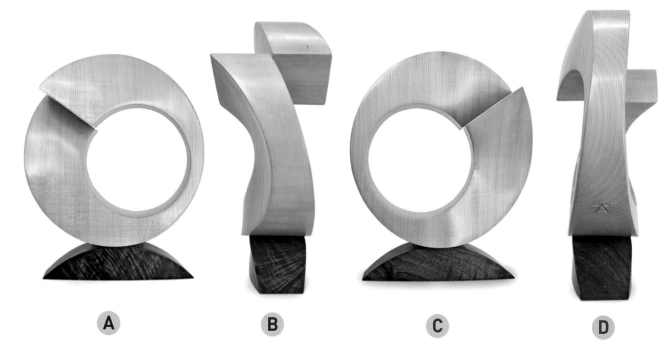

A   B   C   D

THE CARVING

Before you start working on the piece, read through the step guide to see how the form develops and study pictures **A**–**D** above to familiarize yourself with the finished form that you are aiming to produce.

Note that the widest point of the form is the cut line where the two circles separate. This is the original depth/thickness of the block. From this position, on both sides, the mass thins as it flows down the edges and then gets wider again at the base, which is approximately two-thirds of the depth/thickness of the widest point. You will be carving four separate corners of the form to produce the flowing shape of the design.

Your first job is to measure and mark a center line on the inner edge of your wood, at the base of the inner circle. This lowest position of the circle will finish at about two-thirds the width of the position where the two parts of the circle separate. This measurement can also be marked on the wood now. For example, if the thickness of your wood is the same as the one in this example, 4½in (114mm), then mark the center line at 2¼in (57mm). Measure out from this center line 1½in (40mm) on both sides to give you the two-thirds you require. The one here is rounded off to 1⅜in (35mm). Picture **8** on page 94 shows this completed.

1 First, study **D** to help you to understand the angle that you are trying to achieve on the left edge of the wood. This is a subtle curve, flowing from the outer edge at the point of the separation that sweeps gently in towards the center and then out again to meet the lowest position you marked previously. You may need to enlist a spare pair of hands to help you draw the line while you hold the flexible rule in position.

2 (See **A** and **D**.) Use the No. 3/30 to carve the wood carefully back to the line. If you feel any resistance in your cut then you are likely to be cutting against the grain. Either change direction of the cut or work across the grain (**2a** and **2b**).

3 This area has now been carved.

4 (See **A**, **B** and **D**.) Study **B** to help you understand the angle you are trying to achieve on this edge of the wood. Measure and mark a center line between the widest part of the wood at the position of the cut where it separates. Use the flexible rule again to draw the curved

1

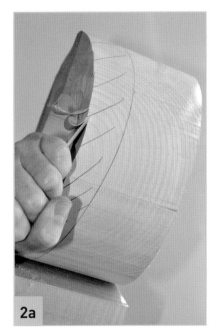

2a

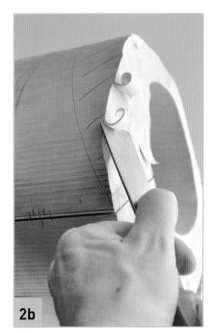

2b

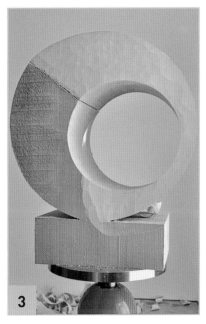

3

4

5

line between this center position down to the lowest position, which should join up level with the outer-edge surface that you have just carved on the opposite face.

5 (See **A**, **B** and **D**.) Use your No. 3/30 to pare the wood back to the line, following the suggested cutting directions as marked.

6 The upper position has been carved into the center line, and the lower position has been carved back to the two-thirds line, evenly joining the opposite face to complete this side.

7 (See **B**, **C** and **D**.) Moving onto the opposite edge, use the flexible ruler again and mark a more acute curve here, running from the outer edge down to the two-thirds line.

8 Mark a line on the inner edge (not as acute as the one on the outer edge), so that the wood will taper out slightly when carved.

6

7

8

9a

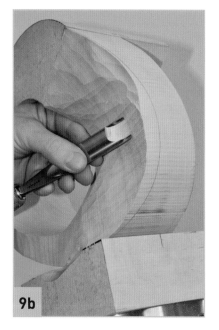

9b

9 (See **B**, **C** and **D**.) Use the No. 3/30 to pare the wood back to the inner and outer lines 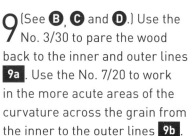. Use the No. 7/20 to work in the more acute areas of the curvature across the grain from the inner to the outer lines **9b**.

10 (See **A**, **B**, **C** and **D**.) With this edge completed, you can now clearly see the slight taper of the mass between the inner and outer edges.

11 (See **C** and **D**.) This final quarter of the design has to be approached with some caution, as the wood will flex a little when you carve it. You must be conscious of the amount of pressure that you apply to your cuts and brace the wood where possible to minimize any chance of it breaking. Study **D** to see the angle of the line that you need to produce. This curves from the center line at the top down to the two-thirds mark at the base. Draw this on your wood with the aid of your flexible rule.

12 Fortunately, the grain on this side of the form is lending itself here, so the pressure and direction of the cut can be made towards the separation in the circle, which will naturally brace this more flexible side against the opposite one. Use your No. 3/30 to work down to the contour line in the direction of the arrows.

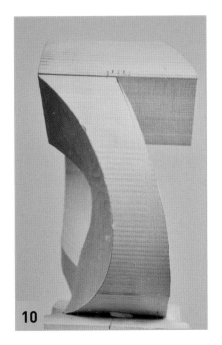

10

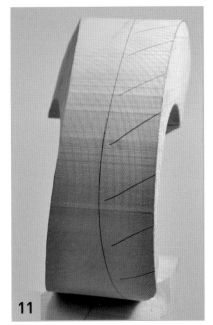

11

12

13

14

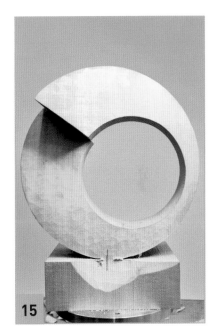

15

13 When you work up to the top position where the wood separates you will need to be careful not to make any deep cuts into the edge on the opposite side, as these could persist when you sand it and be visible when polished. A good tip is to use a piece of dense cardboard folded around the opposite edge of the wood,

thereby protecting it from the cuts and enabling you to finish the shaping of the top edge without any concerns.

14 Your sculpture should now be carved on all areas of its surface and is almost ready for sanding. However, before you start the sanding process, it is good practice to skim over

the surface of the wood with the No. 3/30 to level out any uneven areas or deeper gouge marks. The flusher the surface is, the quicker and easier the sanding procedure will be.

15 The surface has now been skimmed over as smoothly as possible with the No. 3/30 and is ready for sanding.

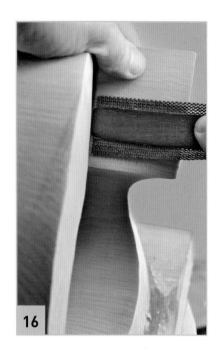

Sanding

Start with 100-grit Abranet and work over the complete surface of the sculpture, following the line of the grain, and completely remove every tool mark.

16 You may find that using a thin piece of wood helps to brace the sandpaper, giving you a stronger action and an appropriate flat edge when sanding the two square edges where the wood separates.

17 To sand the base of the circle on both edges you will need to cut away these marked areas to gain better access.

18 After you have worked over the complete surface with the 100-grit, scrutinize it in good light to make sure that there are no little pits or bumps. A good tip is to turn the sculpture around slowly and study the surface as the shadows strike over it.

This will expose any little lumps and bumps to the meticulous eye. When you are sure that it is perfectly smooth, clean the sawdust off all of the surfaces and then brush or pour hot water over the complete sculpture and leave it to dry. This will raise the grain and allow the subsequent grit to be worked more easily and effectively (for more on the hot-water technique, see page 63).

Next, work through grits 150, 240 and 400, removing all of the scratches from each previous grit and repeating the hot-water technique in between each one. Finally, use a very fine-grit disc (see page 59 for details) to polish the surface up to a fine sheen ready for finishing.

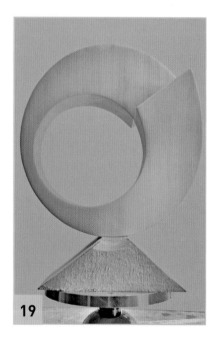

19 The sculpture has now been completely sanded through all the grits and can be cut off the base. Do this very carefully, allowing yourself an extra ⅛in (2–3mm) to be on the safe side. This can then be sanded back through all of the grits flush to the correct contour of the form.

20a

20b

Finishing with wax polish

The simplest way to finish a sculpture is with a couple of applications of wax polish straight onto the surface of the wood. You will need to purchase a clear wax that actually seals the grain of the wood, gives some degree of protection against ultra-violet rays and, of course, works effectively as a polish. Your supplier will give you advice on the best one to buy.

20 Different polishes have different techniques for effective application. Some need to be applied and then left for 20 minutes; others require even longer. With quick-drying waxes it is important to apply the wax to small areas of around 4–6in (100–150mm) at a time, give it a quick blow to dry the surface and

then buff it off with a soft cloth, all within about 30 seconds to a minute. Carefully following the instructions on the packaging of your wax, work over the complete surface of your sculpture, then repeat the process once more to give it a wonderful finish.

Base

A piece of American black walnut measuring H 1½ x W 7 x D 2½in (38 x 178 x 64mm) has been selected for the base. It was chosen for the complementary contrast between the two woods and because the darker color sits quietly underneath the lime in the shadows. All of its edges reflect the gentle curves of the Wave, and it is slightly smaller in size from both profile views, giving it a good balance that sits

well on the eye and works in harmony with the sculpture. If you would like to make the same base as this in a wood of your choice, then have a go at drawing it yourself, using picture **21** as a reference. It then simply needs to be cut out, sanded through grits 100, 150, 240, 400 and finally with the fine-grit disc. You will need to drill two holes in the center of the piece from the top, and countersink from underneath. The sculpture can then be held in position carefully and fixed with screws.

Finishing

When working with dark woods, it is effective to apply a fine coat of boiled linseed oil (please read the warning on page 109). This enriches the color of the wood, making it darker and enhancing the figure of the grain (see **21**). It should be left to dry for at least one week before applying a dark wax polish – this will produce a wonderful sheen and protect it from ingraining dust discoloration and ultra-violet rays.

Finally, cover the bottom of the base with self-adhesive black baize to protect both it and the surfaces on which it will be placed from damage. Place the base on the baize and draw around its shape. Cut it out, peel off the paper and stick it to the wood, taking care not to pull it, otherwise it will stretch and won't fit flush with the edge.

21

FOSSIL

Difficulty level: 3/10 on the beginner's scale

Time to complete: 15–25 hours

THE ESSENCE OF THIS SCULPTURE REFLECTS THE SPIRIT OF THE JURASSIC COAST, WHICH IS NEAR WHERE I LIVE IN DORSET, ENGLAND. THE PIECE EMBODIES THE ELEMENTS OF THE COAST'S NATURAL HISTORY: THE FOSSILS, SEASHELLS AND THE SEA. IT IS FULL OF MOVEMENT YET HAS SUBTLE FLOWING CONTOURS.

This project is a progression from the previous project, Wave. The center ellipse is not cut with a bandsaw and therefore must be produced by hand with a drill and gouges. The edges of the sculpture are curved as opposed to the straight edges of Wave. Patience and time are required to create the gentle flowing contour evenly around the complete outer edge, and the angled edge that connects the top of the sculpture with the ellipse will test and improve your control skills with the introduction of the V-Tool.

TOOLS

No. 3/30
No. 7/20
No. 5/20 (new for this project)
No. 12/10 (new for this project)
Drill bit – $\frac{5}{32}$in (4mm)
Brad-point drill bit
Bradawl

WOOD

English walnut

Dimensions before cutting profile: H 13 x W 8 x D 3in (330 x 203 x 76mm)

Dimensions of Fossil: H 11¼ x W 7¼ x D 2⅞in (286 x 185 x 73mm)

This sculpture is made from English walnut, which is a much harder wood than the lime used in the previous project and far more unforgiving if you attempt to carve it against the grain.

What you will learn

- How to make a large piercing or hole in your sculpture
- How to use a V-Tool (No. 12)
- How to approach awkward grain
- How to carve a cylindrical form
- How to secure the sculpture to the base accurately in an upright position
- How to finish the sculpture with boiled linseed oil

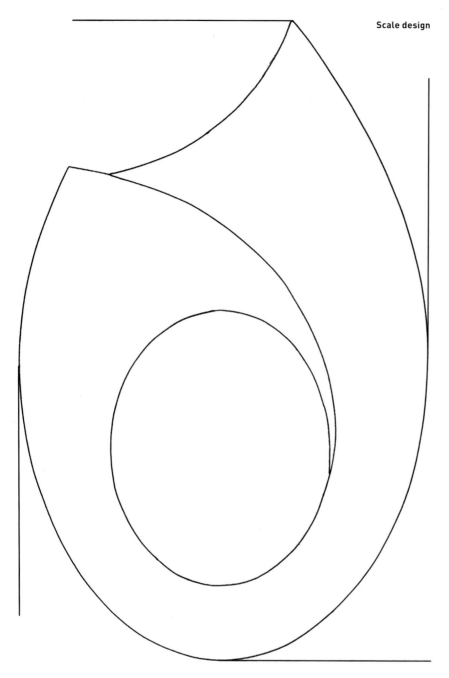

Scale design

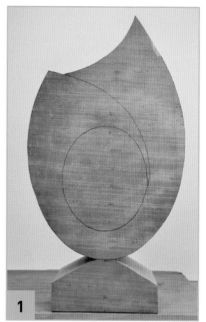

SCALE DESIGN AND CUTTING OUT

1 Scan or photocopy the scale drawing provided, enlarging it to the correct size for your wood. Print it out onto card, and use it as a template to transfer the design onto the front and back sides of your prepared block, with the grain running vertically up through the design. Cut it out, either with a bandsaw or by hand, following the procedures outlined on pages 78–81, as well as in the Wave project (see pages 90–91).

2 Remove the wood from the inner ellipse of the form. As with Wave (see page 91), use a large brad-point drill bit to make a series of adjoining drill holes around the line of the ellipse until you go full circle and the center pops out. Drill as close to the line as comfortably possible, but do not overlap the drill holes by too much, otherwise the bit will attempt to follow the previous hole. When complete, mount the block securely onto your vise.

A   B   C   D

THE CARVING

Before you start working on the piece, read through the step guide to see how the form develops and study pictures **A**-**D** above to familiarize yourself with the finished form that you are aiming to produce.

1 Before you start carving around the inner ellipse, you must make sure that the design corresponds correctly on both sides of the form. Use your original template as a reference, and make adjustments if need be. Carefully following the line, carve in towards the center of the sculpture from both sides, removing the sharp edges left by the drill bit and taking the depth back flush and neat to the ellipse line. Do this using the No. 7/20 for the more acute curve at the top and bottom and the No. 5/20 in between.

1

2

If you have already completed Wave, the first thing that you will notice is how hard walnut is compared with lime, particularly on the end grain at the top and bottom of the ellipse. Make sure that you strop your gouges regularly to keep their cutting edges razor sharp. If necessary, use a mallet to assist you.

2 Using your flexible rule, measure and draw a center line onto the wood around both the inner ellipse and the outer edges of the sculpture.

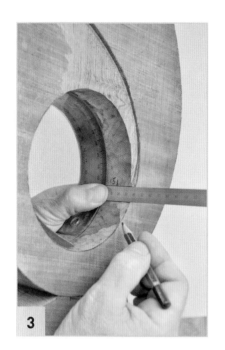

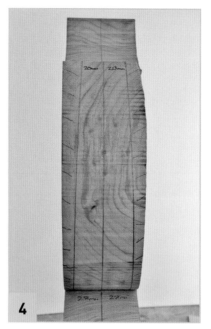

3 Draw a horizontal line squarely across the inner ellipse connecting the two sides at the point where the ellipse blends into the outer line. Measure ⅝in (15mm) out from the center line and mark this on both sides of the horizontal line. This is the position to which the inner ellipse will eventually be carved back.

4 (See **B**.) Moving to the top of the outer edge, measure ¾in (20mm) out from the center line on both sides and mark this position onto your wood. Then at the bottom of the outer edge, measure 1⅛in (28mm) out from the center line on both sides and mark these positions. Use the flexible rule to join these two positions together and mark them.

5 Moving back to the inner ellipse again, you need to draw a line that spirals out from the ⅝in (15mm) marked position, upwards and around the ellipse, corresponding to the same angle and depth of the lines that you have just marked on the outer edge of the wood. Use the flexible rule again to assist you.

6 (See **A**.) Use the No. 12/10 V-Tool to carve a groove directly underneath the line, from the side of the ellipse up to the top of the form.

TIP The 10mm No. 12 V-Tool is a very useful size for most applications. The main thing to remember when using this tool is that it has a tendency to slip when applied under pressure, so be aware of this and make sure that you start with shallow cuts when first following a line. After you have made an initial channel, then you can add more pressure as the tool will be less likely to slip in the groove that it has produced. One other point to note is that because of the V-shape end of the tool, you will find that when you make repeated cuts you will inadvertently move away from your original line. Be aware of this, and keep checking against your original template and redraw the line if necessary. You can then hold the V-Tool flat on its shoulder and cut back towards the original line again.

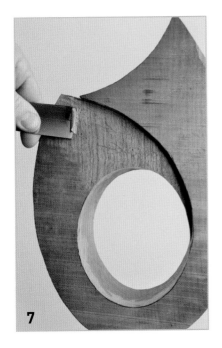

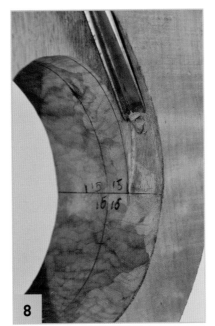

9 (See **A** and **B**.) Moving to the left of the ellipse on the same side, use the No. 3/30 to pare the wood evenly back to the line on the edge of the wood that you drew earlier in step 4.

10 (See **A**.) As you work down to the middle position of the curve on the left edge, you will need to change your direction of cut downwards to follow the grain pattern correctly.

11 Your sculpture should now look like this.

7 (See **A**.) Use the No. 3/30, working horizontally across the grain, to pare away the wood down to the depth of (but no lower than) the V-Tool groove.

8 (See **A**.) Repeat steps 6 and 7 until you reach the line of the spiral that you drew earlier in step 5.

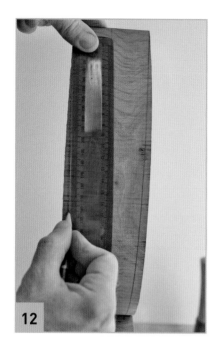

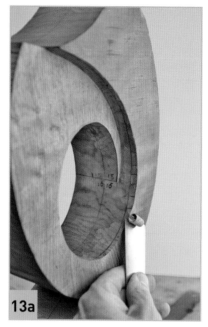

12 (See **D**.) Next, move to the area right of the ellipse. Working on the opposite outer edge of the wood and starting at the base, measure 1⅛in (28mm) out from the center line on both sides and mark these positions on your wood. Use your flexible rule to join these positions up to the full width of the top outer edges.

13 (See **A**, **B** and **D**.) You now need to extend the spiral line, which you drew in step 5, outwards and upwards from the lowest position of the ellipse to the top of the line that emerges from the ellipse that you formed in steps 6 and 7.

Use the No. 3/30 to pare away the wood back to these inner and outer lines **13a**, following the direction of cut suggested by the arrows drawn on the wood here **13b**. At the lowest position of the sculpture, where the contour of the Fossil joins the base, you will need to use your No. 7/20 to pare the wood back to the 1⅛in (28mm) line that you marked in steps 4 and 12.

14 Your sculpture should now look like this.

Repeat steps 5–13 on the opposite side of your wood.

15 (See **D**.) Now move to the outer edges of the sculpture, which are naturally curved from one side to the other around the complete sculpture. These contours are simple in their shape but need to be formed with care to create a fully rounded edge. If you take too much mass away from these edges, you will create a more pointed area in the center; conversely, if you don't take enough away, it will look square. Draw this curve on the upper edge of your wood.

16 (See **C** and **D**.) Use the No. 3/30 to pare the upper edge back to your marked line, carving horizontally across the grain. Then use the same gouge upside down, so that the curvature of the tool is lending itself to the curve that you are aiming to produce, and work vertically upwards to round over the edge, following the same contour as you made at the top.

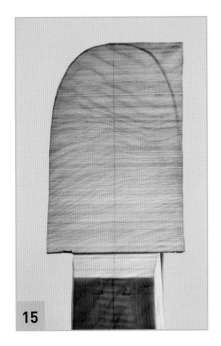

15

16

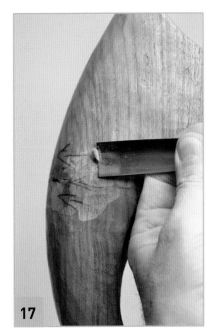

17

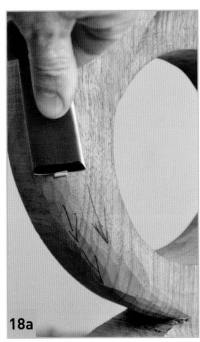

18a

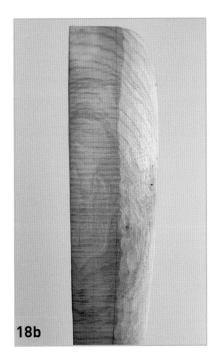

18b

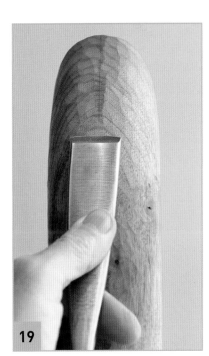

19

17 (See **C** and **D**.) Continue this curve down to the widest position of the arc on this edge. Because of the grain direction at this point, you will need to use the No. 5/20 to carve across the grain again until you work down past the center of the arc.

18 (See **C** and **D**.) When you are past the center of the outer arc, the grain will allow you to carve vertically downwards along the edge **18a**, continuing the cylindrical contour over this part of the sculpture **18b**.

19 (See **D**.) Now repeat steps 16–18 on the opposite side.

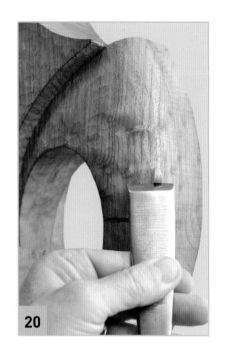

20

21

22a

22b

20 (See **B** and **C**.) Moving over to the opposite edge, draw another curve on the top if you wish, or just work carefully with the No. 3/30 held upside down again, carving vertically along this edge to produce the cylindrical contour until you reach the widest position of the arc. Blend the contour of the edge evenly together with the area above the ellipse that you carved in steps 6–11.

21 (See **B** and **C**.) You may need to cut horizontally across the grain here with the No. 5/20, but the grain on the sculpture in the example here meant it was possible simply to merge the depths together without splitting and continue curving the mass downwards over the edge. Either way, after finishing with the No. 5/20, use the No. 3/30 to continue the contour evenly down the edge. Repeat steps 20 and 21 on the opposite side.

22 (See **A**, **B**, **C** and **D**.) The position at the very base of the sculpture will now need to be cut in towards the center, both from the front and back (**A** and **C**), so that the contour that you produced on the edge of the form can be continued evenly all the way around the bottom edge.

The curvature of the No. 3/30 is perfect for this task. Simply place it in position on the bottom line of the form **22a** and either gently tap with a mallet or push firmly into the wood and rock from side to side to produce the cut. The No. 5/20 is then used to undercut into this No. 3 cut, taking the depth of the mass further in towards the center **22b**. This procedure should be repeated on both sides until there is approximately ⅝in (15mm) of mass underneath in the center to hold the sculpture onto the base. The No. 3/30 is then used again to continue

shaping the contour of the edge down both sides, eventually meeting at the base in the middle.

23 Your sculpture should now be completely formed. It is good practice at this point to examine the surface areas carefully for any bumps or undulations that may need to

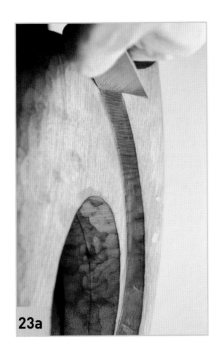

23a

23b

24

be tweaked slightly and made smooth and flat before you attempt to sand them. Examine the sculpture in natural light, turning it slowly and observing the shadows casting over the surface, which will expose any uneven areas for you to tidy.

Other areas to clean up before sanding will include the flat area of the line emerging from the ellipse **23a** and the bandsaw marks on the top of the sculpture **23b**. Use the No. 3/30 and the No. 5/20 to do these jobs.

24 The surfaces of the sculpture have now been tidied up and are ready to be sanded.

Sanding

25 To facilitate the sanding procedure, the sculpture is left on its base and is worked through all the grits, using the hot-water technique in between each one (see page 63).

26 When you have completely sanded all the surfaces of the sculpture, carefully cut it off its base as tight to the line of its contour as possible. Next, sand this edge using 100-grit Abranet to blend all of the depths evenly together, then continue through all grits, using the hot-water technique in between each one.

Base

27 The base shown here is a simple segment of an arc, which looks very effective with both contours of the base and sculpture blending away from one another, giving the visual impression that the sculpture is balanced freely on the base.

The wood used is American black walnut, and it measured H ¾ x W 6 x D 1½in (20 x 153 x 38mm) before cutting. A ⁵⁄₃₂in (4mm) brad-point drill bit was used to drill the center hole, which was then countersunk from underneath. A bandsaw was used to cut the arc to shape. You can copy this base if you wish, but why not try to experiment with your own design to personalize your sculpture?

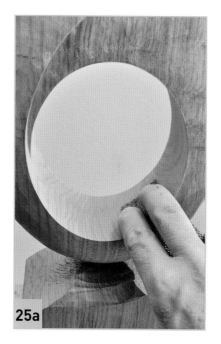

25a

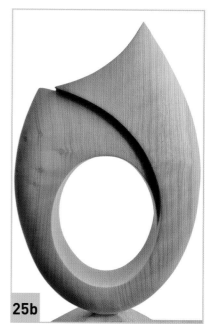

25b

26

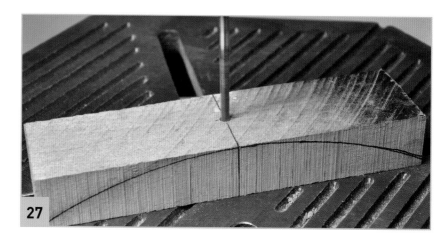

27

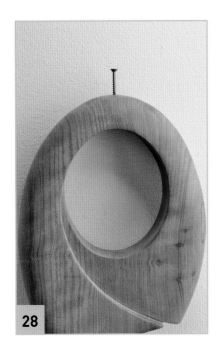

28 Mounting your sculpture on to your base has to be done with care and precision to ensure that it is perfectly upright without listing in any direction. An accurate way to do this is to measure and mark the exact position where the base of the sculpture will be attached. Make a small hole with a bradawl and then slowly insert a screw into the hole, checking its angle from all positions at every turn and moving it if necessary. You can then remove the screw, mount the sculpture on the base and carefully secure them together to display the sculpture in a perfect upright position.

WARNING! If you are using boiled linseed oil, read the warnings on the container very carefully, as the cloths you use are prone to spontaneous combustion if you do not dispose of them properly.

Finishing

29 The completed sculpture on page 99 was finished with a very thin application of boiled linseed oil to darken and enrich the grain of the wood. It was then left for a week before applying a dark wax polish.

Use a small soft cloth that measures approximately 2 x 2in (50 x 50mm) to apply the oil. Do not soak the cloth or the sculpture with the oil but add just enough for it to penetrate the grain and color the surface. If you do use too much, it can take a very long time to dry out and can also clog details or corners, which will then need to be scraped out. If there is any excess on the surface after application, then simply wipe it off immediately with a dry cloth. This will eliminate any further problems.

Finally, after allowing a week for the oil to dry, give the wood two coats of dark wax polish. This will produce a lovely sheen on the surface and really give depth to, and enhance the rays and figuring of, the grain.

CAT

Difficulty level: 4/10 on the beginner's scale

Time to complete: 15–25 hours

THIS STYLIZED CAT IS REALLY FUN AND SIMPLE TO PRODUCE. YOU WILL BE USING HOLLOWS AND CONTOURS TO GIVE THE IMPRESSION OF THE UNDERLYING VOLUMES OF THE LEGS, TAIL AND SURFACE ANATOMY, LEAVING JUST THE EARS CLOSE TO THEIR REAL-LIFE APPEARANCE.

In the early stages of learning woodcarving, one of the most common miscalculations is to be overly cautious when establishing the main form of the subject, thus creating a form that is too square looking. It is vital that you gather as much reference material as possible to give you a clear visual understanding of the form that you are trying to reproduce. This will help you to solve any problems with the surface anatomy and give you the confidence to understand that you are not taking too much of the mass away. To help you with this, study images of cats from all angles, preferably in the same upright seated posture as the subject that you are carving. The study and observation of a living cat will also be advantageous.

TOOLS

No. 3/30
No. 5/20
No. 7/20
No. 7/6 (new for this project)
No. 9/10 (new for this project)

WOOD

Tulipwood (North American)

Dimensions before cutting profiles: H 10 x W 5 x D 3½in (254 x 127 x 89mm)

Dimensions of Cat: H 8¼ x W 4 x D 3¼in (210 x 102 x 82mm)

Tulipwood is quite hard in density to carve, but it is far more forgiving than the English walnut that was used for the previous project, Fossil. It also has a beautiful grain figuring with the outer sapwood being a light tan and the heartwood various shades of olive green.

What you will learn

- How to shape the form
- How to create the cat's ears, eyes, legs and tail
- How to check for symmetry
- How to create the illusion of abstracted realism

Scale design

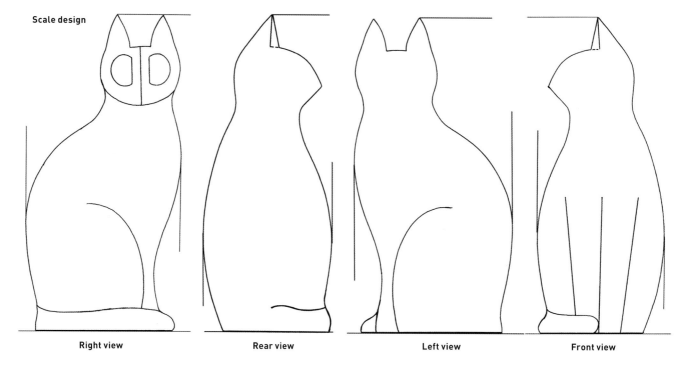

| Right view | Rear view | Left view | Front view |

SCALE DESIGN AND CUTTING OUT

1 Scan or photocopy the scale drawings provided, enlarging them to the correct size for your wood. Print them out onto card and use them as templates to transfer the front- and side-view profiles accurately onto the front and side of your prepared block. Use a square to ensure that both profiles are in perfect alignment with each other.

2 Cut both profiles, following the same procedures outlined on pages 78–81, then attach the form securely to your vise.

GOLDEN RULE It is important to make sure that your two profiles are both applied to the wood facing in the correct direction otherwise your form will be cut in the exact mirror image of what you had intended.

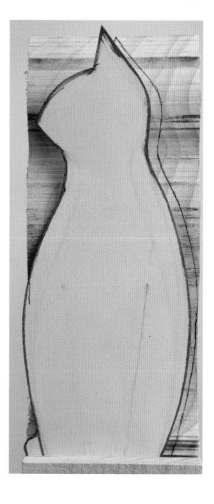

TIP To help simplify the shaping around the lower edges of the cat, it is beneficial to cut along the horizontal lines at the very bottom edge, as if you were going to cut it off the base, but stopping at about ¾in (20mm) before the center of the cat on all sides, leaving the form attached to the base by a 1½in (40mm) square section underneath it. This will enable you to carve easily around the lower edges of the body without the need to carve into the square base, saving you time and energy in those areas. You can see this clearly in picture **13** on page 117.

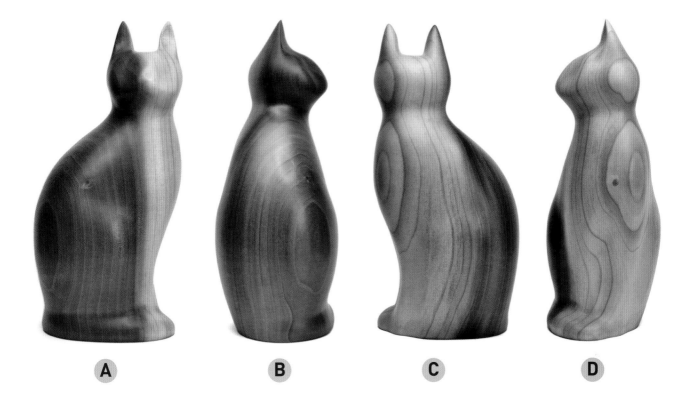

A   **B**   **C**   **D**

THE CARVING

Before you start working on the piece, read through the step guide to see how the form develops and study pictures **A**–**D** above to familiarize yourself with the finished form that you are aiming to produce.

Head

1 (See **A**, **B** and **D**.) Your first job is to measure and mark the center lines onto all sides of the wood. Now measure ¼in (6mm) out from both sides of the center line on the face and mark these positions on your wood. Use the right-view template as a reference to help you draw the shape of the head onto the wood.

Use the No. 5/20, working horizontally across the grain, to carve the wood back to these lines.

2 (See **A**, **B** and **D**.) Use your No. 3/30 to round over the straight edges of the face, naturally blending the depths up to the ears, down under the chin and around to the sides of the head.

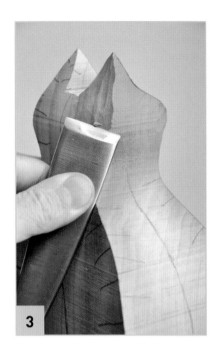

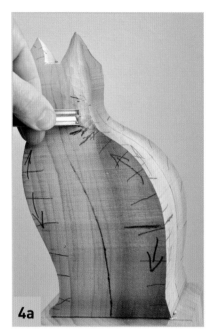

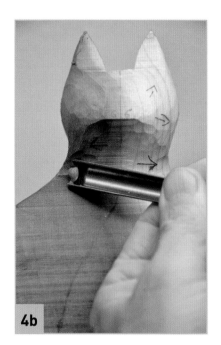

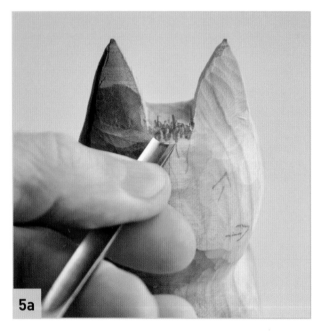

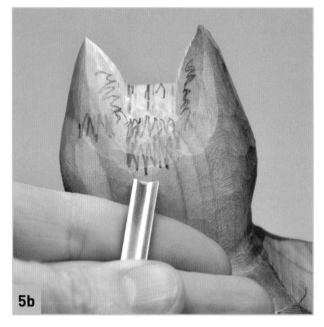

3 (See **B**, **C** and **D**.) Turn the sculpture around and use the No. 3/30 again to curve the edges of the back of the head across from the center line, up over the ears and around onto the side of the head. You should now be able to merge the front and back of the head evenly together.

4 (See **A**, **B**, **C** and **D**.) When you have worked your way down the front and back of the head to the position of the neck **4a**, you will need to use the No. 9/10, working horizontally across the grain, to create a gentle flowing curve right around the complete contour of the neck **4b**. These deeper gouge cuts will need to be blended evenly into the surrounding areas, up onto the head and down onto the body. Do this with the No. 7/6.

5 (See **A**, **B**, **C** and **D**.) The only remaining flat area on the head is between the cat's ears. Use the No. 7/6 again, to curve the back and front of the head, up onto the peak of **5a**. The ears can then be shaped,

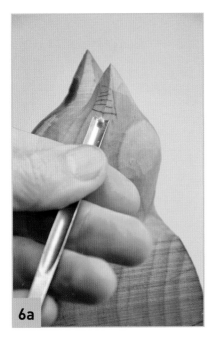

6a

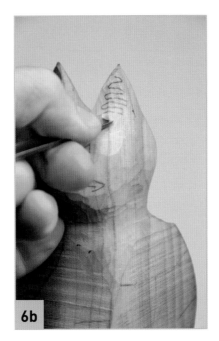

6b

7

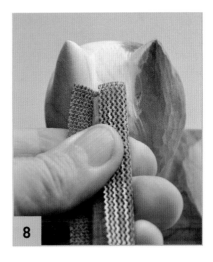

8

curving them from the very back in towards the center of the head, removing the inner square edge and bringing them to life **5b** . To help you understand this detail, use your reference material as a guide.

Ear shape

6 (See **A**, **B** and **D**.) The effect that you are trying to achieve here is to move the outer edge of the ears back about ¼in (6mm) on the side of the head from that of the inner edge, in order to reflect one of the many positions of a living cat's ears.

Measure ¼in (6mm) back from the front outer edge of the ear and mark this in position **6a** . Use the No. 7/6 to pare the wood back to this line **6b** .

7 (See **A**, **B** and **D**.) You now need to carve the concave hollow into the ear between its outer and inner edges. Do this using the No. 7/6 again, making shallow cuts horizontally across the ear and carving as deep as your gouge will allow.

8 Before carving the hollowed position of the eyes, sand over the entire surface of the head with 100-grit to blend all of the contours completely and evenly together. When you have done this, closely scrutinize all of the contours on both sides of the head from several different angles to ensure that they are symmetrical. If necessary, make adjustments and re-sand it.

When checking for the correct symmetry of contoured areas such as the cat's head, the best method is first to look from above, down through the face, and then do the same from below, looking up through

the face. The form is moved vertically back and forth, focusing on the center line and using your peripheral vision to check for symmetry.

TIP If you wrap a piece of your sandpaper around a flat stick, it can be used effectively to shape and blend the ears and their surrounding areas together.

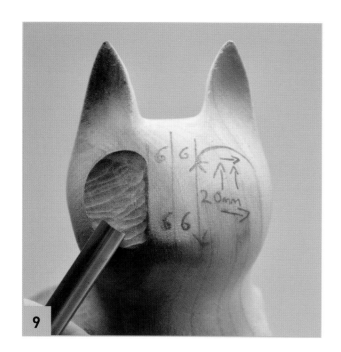

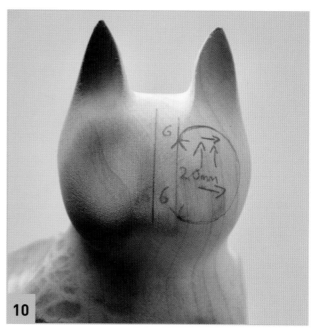

Eyes

9 (See **A**, **B** and **D**.) The effect you need to produce here is created simply by carving a hollow where the eyes are located, up to the side of the nose. When the sculpture is finished, the shadows will fall in these hollows creating an abstracted realism around the eyes and nose.

Use the right-view scale drawing as a reference to help you apply the following details onto your wood. Redraw the center line back up through the face. Measure ¼in (6mm) out from both sides of the center line at the top and bottom of it and draw a line up through the face in both of these positions. Measure ¾in (20mm) up from the position of the nose and mark this on the ¼in (6mm) lines. Measure ¾in (20mm) out from both sides of the center line and mark these on your wood. Draw the positions of the hollowed area, as in the right-view scale drawing, curving out from the ¼in (6mm) line at the upper position, out to the ¾in (20mm) line and back down into the lower position at the ¼in (6mm) line.

Now use the No. 7/6, working horizontally across this area, to carve the hollow to a depth of approximately ⅛in (2–3mm) in the center.

10 (See **A**, **B** and **D**.) Sand the complete area with 100-grit, smoothing over all of the sharp edges to soften the face completely and blend the depths of the eye and nose naturally together. Repeat steps 9 and 10 on the opposite side.

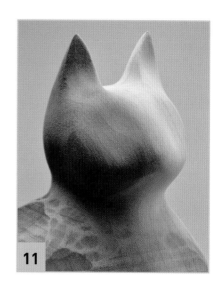

11 You have now completed the head and your sculpture should look like this.

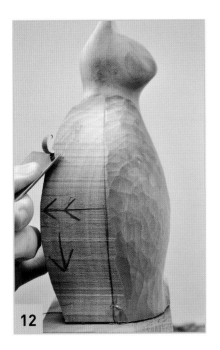

12

13

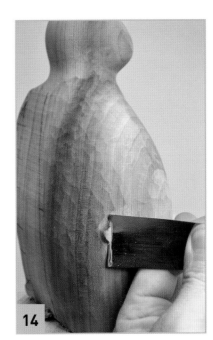

14

Body

12 (See **A**, **B** and **C**.) Next, turn your attention to the body. In the picture you can see the direction of cut that you will need to follow marked. Start on the right side of the upper half, working from the center line on the back around to the center line on the side and up to the neck, blending the contours evenly together at this position. Don't forget that your aim is to create the natural curvature of the cat's back and so you must completely remove any sign of the square edges. Use your reference material to help you to understand these contours before you start, and then carve them using the No. 3/30.

13 (See **A**, **B** and **C**.) Now do the same down the lower part of the back.

14 (See **A**, **B** and **C**.) Finally, blend all of the depths evenly together. Use the No. 3/30, working horizontally across the grain, from the middle position of the arc of the back across to the center line on the sides of the body. Repeat steps 12–14 on the opposite side of the back and then blend both these areas evenly together up the spine. Carefully check for symmetrical balance on both sides of the body as described in step 8 and adjust if necessary.

15 (See **A**, **C** and **D**.) Moving to the front of the body next, the upper shoulders and chest are carved first, in the same way as the back, from the center line on the front, across to the center line on the side and up to the neck. Do this on both sides using the No. 3/30.

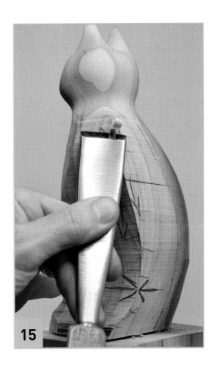

15

16

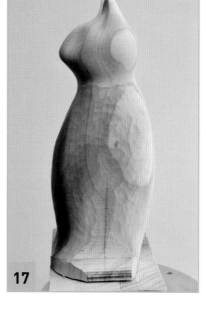

17

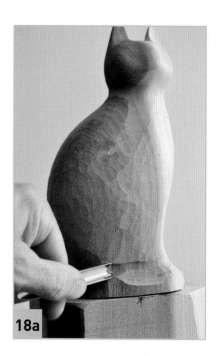

18a

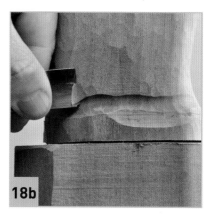

18b

19

16 (See **A**, **C** and **D**.) The lower area of the front body has a tighter curvature where you will shortly be positioning the legs, and it therefore needs to be shaped from the side to the front using the No. 7/20. The No. 5/20 is then used to blend the surrounding depths together evenly.

17 Your sculpture should now look like this.

18 (See **A**, **B** and **D**.) Before you can continue with the cat's legs, you must first carve the tail in its position. The aim here is to give the visual impression of the volume of the tail wrapped around the body, from the base of the back right leg around to the front right paw.

Use the scale drawings to help you measure and draw the tail in its correct position around the form. Use the No. 9/10 to carve a groove directly along the upper edge of its length **18a**, and the No. 5/20 to shape the tail and blend in the depths of the surrounding areas **18b**. The base of the tail should be rounded underneath very slightly, by approximately ⅛in (2–3mm), to give the visual impression of its natural shape. Repeat these procedures until you achieve a naturalistic impression of it.

19 Your tail should now look like this.

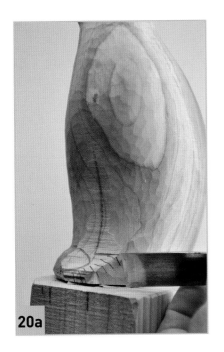

20a

20b

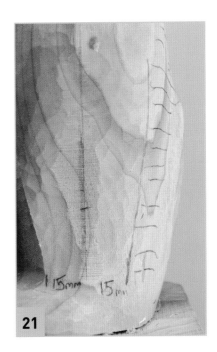

21

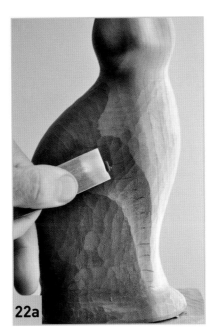

22a

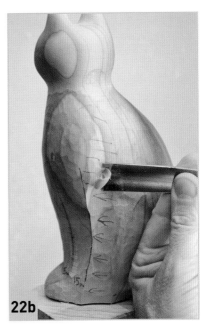

22b

20 (See **A**, **C** and **D**.) The final job to do on the tail is to remove its bandsawn extension in front of the left paw so that it appears just to be curled around the right paw. Use your left-view scale drawing as a reference from which to measure and pare away the mass directly next to the tail and in front of the left paw back in line with the left paw **20a**. Do this with the No. 5/20 and then blend in all of the surrounding areas evenly **20b**.

21 (See **A**, **C** and **D**.) Returning again now to the positioning of the cat's legs, and using the front-view scale drawing as a reference, measure and redraw (if you need to) the center line up through the front view of the cat. Then, at the base of the legs, measure ⅝in (15mm) out from both sides of the center line and mark these positions on your wood. Measure and mark, 3½in (90mm) up from the base to the chest. Measure and mark

1in (25mm) out from this position on both sides of the center line. Draw the tapered line to join up these positions, from the base of the legs up to the chest on both sides. These lines delineate the position of the legs.

22 (See **A**, **B**, **C** and **D**.) Referring to your left- and right-view templates, draw the two hind legs on both sides of the cat in their correct positions. Use the No. 5/20, working horizontally across the grain, to pare away the wood around the shape of the hind legs until you reach the depth of the tapered line you have just positioned **22a**, **22b**.

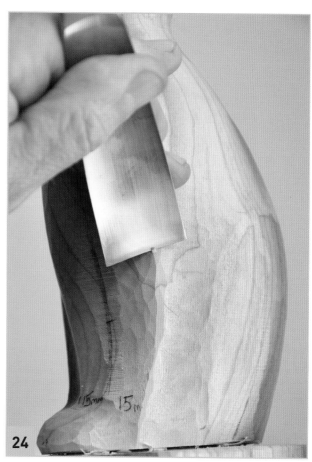

23 (See **A**, **B**, **C** and **D**.) Use the No. 3/30 to blend in the surrounding areas evenly.

24 (See **A**, **C** and **D**.) Use the No. 3/30 to curve the outer edges of the front legs naturally into the contour of the hind legs.

25 (See **D**.) The final job to do on the legs is to create a slight hollow between them where the shadow will naturally fall, enhancing their definition.

Measure approximately ⁵⁄₁₆in (8mm) out from both sides of the center line at the base and mark these positions on your wood. Measure approximately 2¾in (70mm) up from the base and mark this position on your wood.

Measure approximately ⁵⁄₁₆in (8mm) out from both sides of the center line again at the 2¾in (70mm) position and mark these positions on your wood. Draw two vertical lines, joining the lower and higher ⁵⁄₁₆in (8mm) positions together. Use the No. 5/20, working across the grain in between these positions, to carve an even hollow to an approximate depth of ⅛in (2–3mm) in the center.

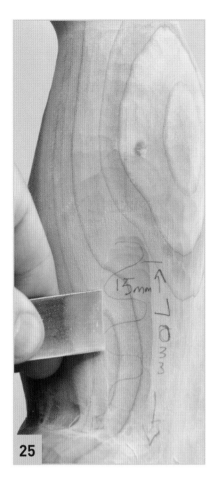

25

Sanding

26 Sand the cat through all the grits, using the hot-water technique in between each one (see page 63). You can then cut it off the base and sand the bottom edges.

Finishing

The Cat on page 111 has been finished using the same method as chosen for Fossil: using boiled linseed oil to enrich the color of the wood and a dark wax on top to seal the grain and give it a good sheen. (See Wave, page 97, for wax polishing instructions and Fossil, page 109, for boiled linseed oil instructions.) You can follow these procedures if you wish or, alternatively, use a finish of your own choice.

26

FEMALE TORSO

Difficulty level: 5/10 on the beginner's scale

Time to complete: 20–30 hours

THE STUDY OF HUMAN FORM IS A SUBJECT THAT HAS OBSESSED ARTISTS SINCE TIME IMMEMORIAL, AND ONE THAT IS NOT ONLY FASCINATING BUT ALSO VERY IMPORTANT TO EXPLORE AND EXPERIMENT WITH AS YOU BEGIN TO DEVELOP YOUR WOODCARVING SKILLS.

Working on the human figure will help you to gain valuable technical and creative experience that is essential to your progression as a woodcarver and it will be of immense value as you work through various different subjects and projects. There are many elements that will bring life to a figurative sculpture, but the most important areas of the design are concept, scale, proportion, posture, movement and harmony. The initial concept portraying the meaning of the sculpture will normally be the dictating factor in the pose and motion of the piece, but it is important that all of the various volumes or structures are carefully balanced with one another to create harmony in the finished piece as a whole.

The human body is an incredibly complex machine with almost infinite degrees of articulation and movement that can be very challenging for the sculptor to capture correctly. So, this is a gentle introduction to the subject with a fairly simple abstracted design that incorporates the correct scale of the human form and has movement in the upper body and the legs.

TOOLS

No. 3/30
No. 7/20
No. 5/20
No. 9/10
Bradawl

WOOD

Lime (basswood)

Dimensions before cutting profiles: H 12 x W 4 x D 3in (305 x 102 x 76mm)

Dimensions of Female Torso: H 10¾ x W 3¾ x D 2½in (273 x 95 x 64mm)

What you will learn

■ How to add movement to a figurative sculpture
■ How to form the basic shape of the human female figure
■ How to abstract certain details
■ How to add the subtle surface anatomy of the breast, abdomen, hips, shoulders, back, buttocks and legs
■ How to add tensions to the medium
■ How to make an appropriate base

GOLDEN RULE You must understand what detail you are trying to achieve before you start working on it.

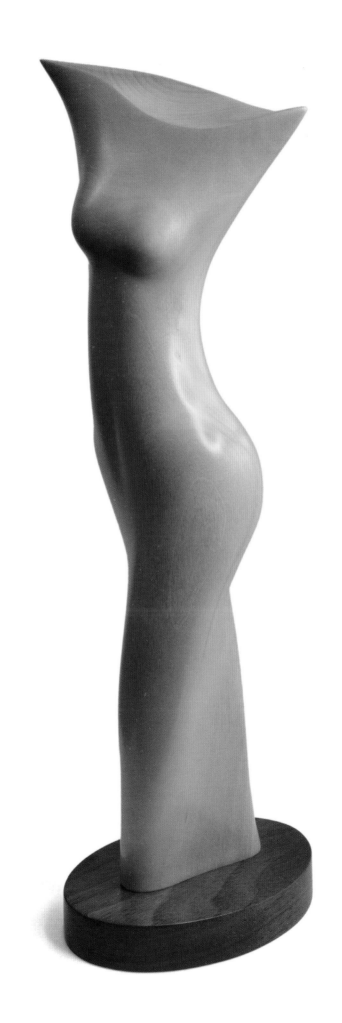

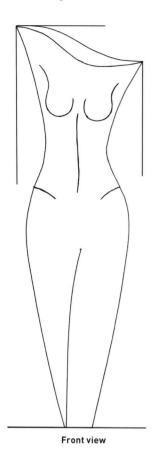
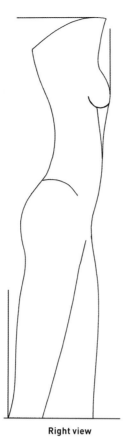

Front view

Right view

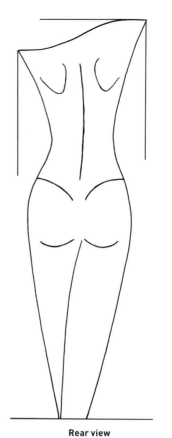
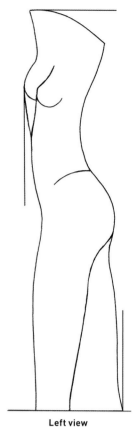

Rear view

Left view

SCALE DESIGN AND CUTTING OUT

Scan or photocopy the scale drawings provided, enlarging them to the correct size for your wood. Print them out onto card and use the front and side views as templates to transfer these two profiles onto the face and side of your prepared block. The other drawings will be used later in the project as a reference. Make sure that they are in precise alignment with one another and that the grain is running vertically up through the design. Cut them out either with a bandsaw or by hand, following the same procedures outlined on pages 78–81. Mount the form securely onto your vise and mark center lines onto each side of the figure.

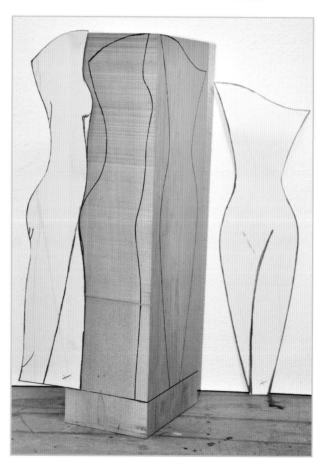

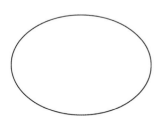

Template for base

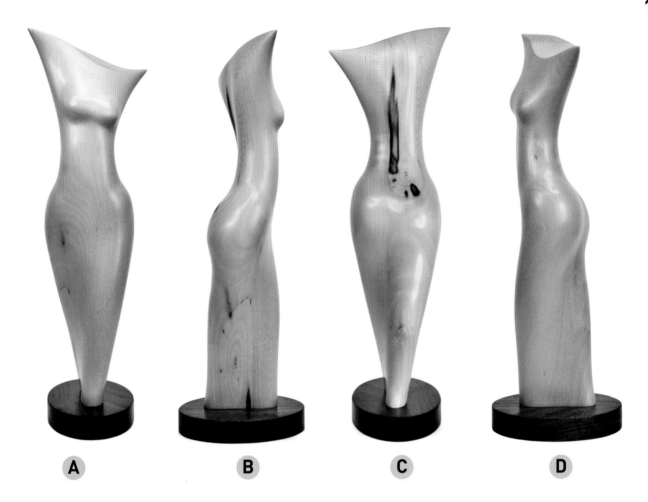

A   B   C   D

THE CARVING

Before you start working on the piece, read through the step guide to see how the form develops and study pictures **A**–**D** above to familiarize yourself with the finished form that you are aiming to produce.

GOLDEN RULE As with almost all figurative work, it is good practice to start shaping the form at the top of the figure, then work your way down methodically through the various details. This is important because the angle of the head will affect the positioning of the shoulders and upper torso, which will in turn affect the angle of the hips and legs.

1 (See **A**, **B**, **C** and **D**.) The first job that you need to do is to create the twist in the upper torso. As well as the pictures of the finished carving, look at **6b** on page 127 to check the angles that you need to create between the left and right shoulders. Draw these curves onto the top of your wood (as shown in **6b**) and use a No. 5/20 to pare the wood away carefully from the front of the right shoulder over the line of the breast to the left shoulder, naturally curving the mass from right to left.

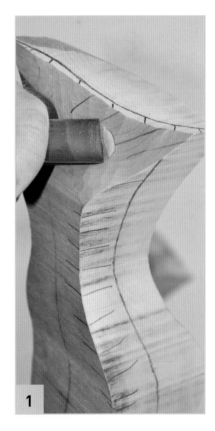

1

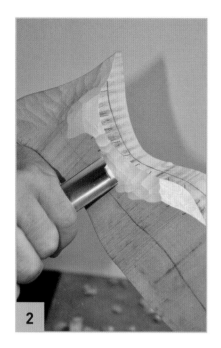

2

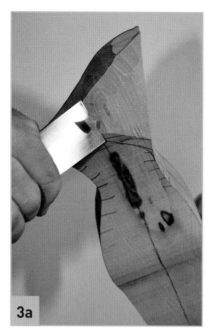

3a

3b

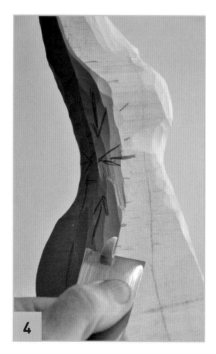

4

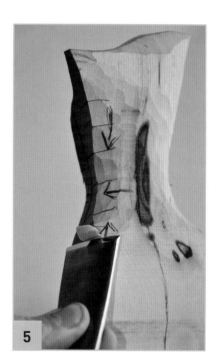

5

2 (See **A** and **D**.) Start rounding over the edge of the body, working down from the shoulder and up from the hip in towards the waistline, using the center lines on the front and side of the figure as a guide. Use a No. 3/30 for working over the hip and breast and a No. 7/20 to work horizontally across the waistline.

3 (See **B** and **C**.) Now turn your figure around and carve the opposite angles on the rear, right-hand side of the body. Again, use **6b** on the facing page as a reference to see the angle that you are trying to create. Carefully pare the wood away using the No. 3/30 from the back of the right shoulder, working from the left shoulder across the back to the right shoulder, naturally curving the mass from left to right **3a**. Then, still using the No. 3/30 along with the No. 7/20, even this depth down the edge of the body from the shoulder and hip in towards the waistline **3b**.

4 (See **A**, **B** and **C**.) You can continue carving this right-hand side of the body on the front side now, repeating the process of carving from the shoulder and hip in towards the waistline, carefully joining the level of depth evenly between the front and back edges.

5 (See **A**, **C** and **D**.) The same can now be done on the rear left-hand side of the body.

6 (See **A**, **B** and **D**.) The angle of the chest now needs to be established and should be carved at the same angle as the shoulders **6b**, reducing the mass mainly across the left breast. Do this with the No. 3/30, but be very careful to leave enough depth to establish the breasts **6a**, **6b**.

7 (See **A**, **B** and **D**.) It is not the intention here to carve realistic breasts, but just to give the correct overall shape to the form in a subtle and smooth, flowing manner. The contours of the breast are quite complex to reproduce, so it would help immensely to study your reference material before you start trying to shape them on your figure.

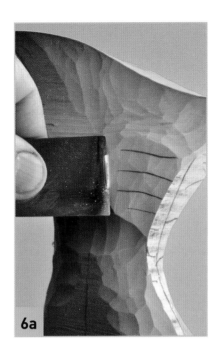

6a

First, use your front-, right- and left-view templates as references to mark the correct positioning of the breasts on your figure. Then use the No. 5/20 to pare away the wood at the top of the breasts onto the upper-chest area, following the direction

6b

of the shaded areas **7a**. Next, use the No. 9/10 to carve around the side and underneath the breasts **7b**, and the No. 5/20 to blend the surrounding areas naturally together **7c**.

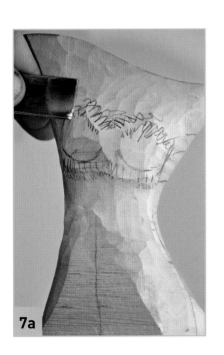

7a

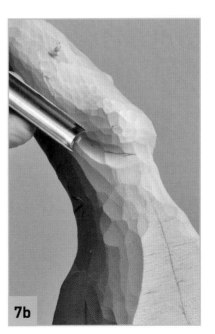

7b

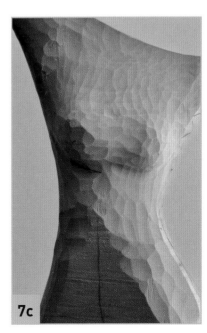

7c

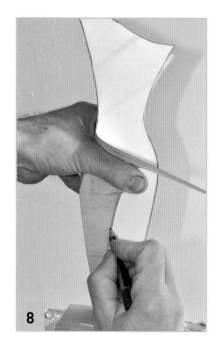

8

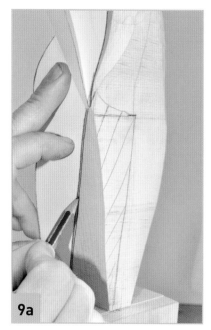

9a

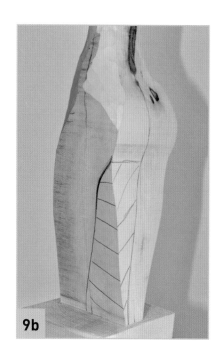

9b

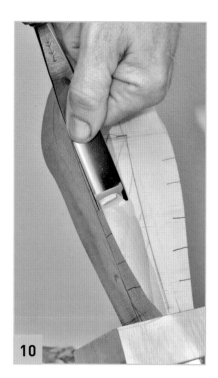

10

8 We now move down to the legs and their positioning. Again, the aim here is not to reproduce realistic legs – more importantly, you are trying to give the impression of the inner structure, or volume, of the leg.

Cut your front-view template along the line of the leg with a pair of scissors. Place it in position on the figure and draw around it onto your wood.

9 Use the same procedure for the side of the right leg **9a** and then again for the back and left side of the left leg **9b**. Use an eraser to rub out the original center lines that you drew and then measure and draw center lines along the face and sides of the legs.

10 (See **A** and **B**.) Use the No. 7/20 to carve away the waste wood between the side of the left leg and the front of the right leg, creating a curved edge between the two.

11 (See **A** and **B**.) Using a No. 5/20 or a No. 3/30 and working from the center positions of the legs, carefully curve over the inner edge of the left leg and the outer edge of the right leg **11a**. If necessary, cut the original line of the right leg again with the No. 7/20 to give more depth to the curve **11b**. Continue the curve of the right leg up over the pelvis and onto the stomach, finally evening up the depth of all of the surrounding areas.

12 (See **A** and **D**.) Next, carve the outer edge of the left leg with the No. 3/30, curving the mass from the center line on the front of the leg to the center line on the side of the leg.

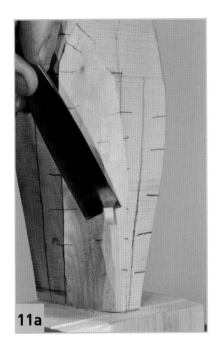

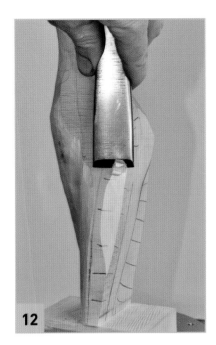

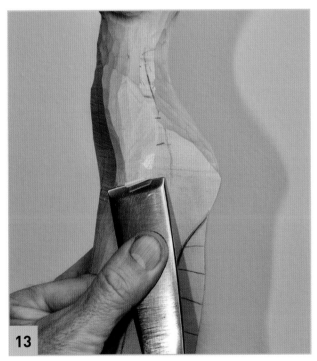

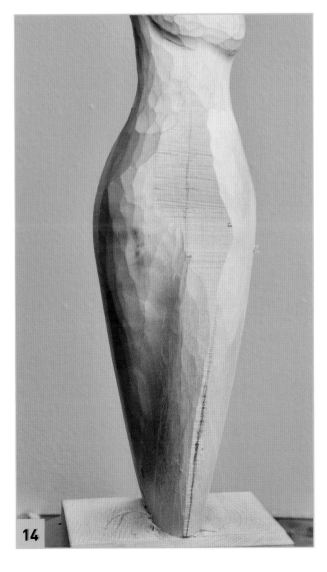

13 (See Ⓐ and Ⓓ.) Continue the curve of the left leg up over the pelvis and onto the stomach before finally evening up the depth of all of the surrounding areas.

14 Your figure should now look something like this.

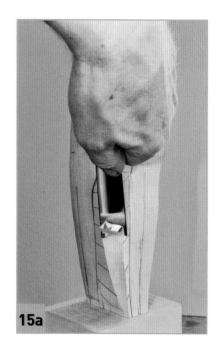

15a

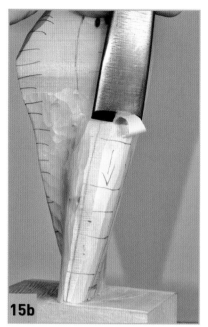

15b

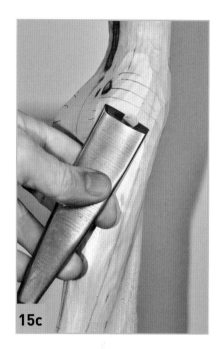

15c

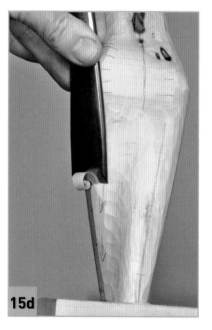

15d

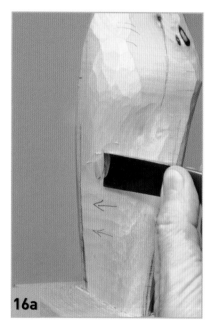

16a

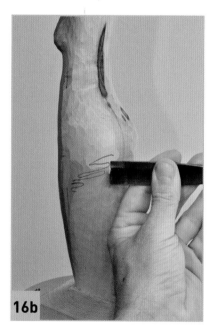

16b

15 (See **B**, **C** and **D**.) Repeat steps 10–13 on the rear of the legs 15a 15b 15c 15d. You may find that the grain is a little tricky in certain areas here. If this is the case, then cut horizontally across it using the No. 5/20.

16 (See **C** and **D**.) The final job you need to do on the legs has to be done very carefully to achieve the correct effect, which is to give the impression that the volume or structure of the legs is within the medium of the wood. This should be similar to the way the legs would appear in a long, tight skirt. The front and sides of the forward-positioned left

leg should show the tensions of the medium around these areas, while the back of the left leg is less noticeable apart from up near the buttock. The backward-positioned right leg is the opposite of this, with the tensions of the medium showing the underlying leg structure more on the sides and back of it but also up on the buttock and pelvis.

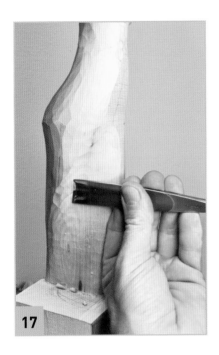

17

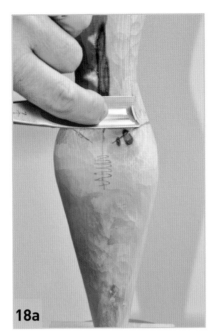

18a

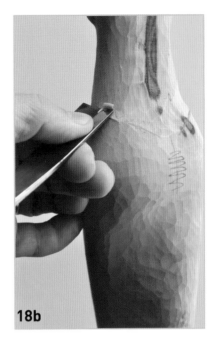

18b

Use your anatomical references and study pictures **C** and **D** to make sure that you understand the detail that you are trying to produce here: the hugging curve around the back of the right leg, which is quite small and tight at the base and sweeps around to the left leg in a slightly concave hollow. As you reach nearer the buttocks the hollow of the curve becomes shallower, giving the impression of the buttocks within the wood.

Use the No. 5/20 to work horizontally across the grain, from near the center line on the back of the right leg, carefully around the back of the right leg across to the center line on the side of the left leg **16a**. As you progress up to the buttock, shorten your cuts more and more towards the back of the left leg (as opposed to the center line on the side of it) and make shallow cuts around its shape to give the impression of its

anatomy on the surface **16b**. If you are unsure whether or not you have cut enough wood away, give the area a quick sanding with 100-grit to see how lifelike the contours appear in the light and shade and make any necessary adjustments.

17 (See **A** and **B**.) Moving to the front position now, this area is approached in the same cautious manner as the back, as you progress up the legs towards the thigh and pelvis. These areas have to show the tensions of the surface anatomy and must be carefully carved to give the impression of the structure of the legs and hips connecting around to the buttocks.

Look closely at **A** and **B** to get an understanding of the delicate contours that you are trying to produce. Use the No. 5/20 to create the concave hollow in the same way as you did on the back of the leg, working from near the

center line on the front of the left leg, around its shape and across to the center line on the side of the right leg. As you work up the leg and approach the level of the thigh, shorten your cuts more and more towards the front of the right leg (as opposed to the cent line on the side of it) and then curve the surface around the thigh and up to the pelvis. Finally, blend in all the surrounding areas together evenly.

18 (See **A**, **B**, **C** and **D**.) Now that you have basically carved the figure in the round, you can add some subtle surface anatomy to help enhance the life of the form. Use your templates as a reference to help you draw the line of the pelvis (iliac crest) onto your wood. Use the No. 7/20 working directly above the lines over the iliac crest, making gouge cuts approximately ⅛in (3mm) deep **18a**. Then use the No. 5/20 to blend the gouge cuts upwards into the back,

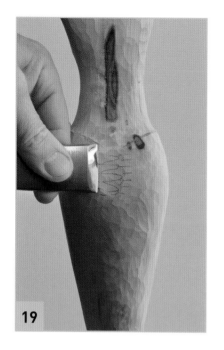

19

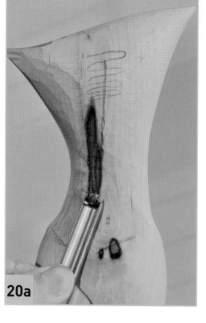

20a

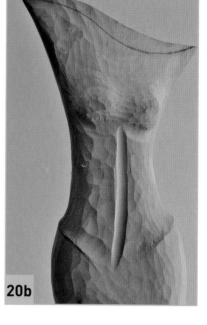

20b

sides and abdomen, leaving the pelvis slightly raised to produce the desired visual effect of the underlying iliac crest bone structure **18b**.

19 (See **C**.) Moving down to the buttocks again, you have to make a slight difference between the depths of the left and right buttock to take into consideration the fact that the left leg is positioned forward, naturally bringing the left buttock slightly forward also. Use the No. 3/30 to pare away approximately ⅛in (2–3mm) off the left buttock, then blend this depth naturally and evenly into the right buttock and also around to the left hip.

20 (See **A** and **C**.) Next, you need to add the grooves on the back and front of the figure to create the visual impression of the muscle separation on the back and stomach areas. Use your front- and rear-view templates to help you measure and draw these lines in their correct positions on the torso. Use the No. 9/10 to cut a groove along these lines and the No. 5/20 to naturally blend the gouge cut into the surrounding areas **20a**, **20b**. The area between the scapulas (shoulder blades) can be opened a little wider with the No. 7/20, to place them into their correct positions.

21 (See **A**.) Finally, you come to the area at the top of the figure, between the shoulders, that needs to be slightly tapered from the back and down towards the front of the sculpture. This will add a finer balance to the visual impression of the figure. Using your front-view template as a reference, draw this curved line onto your wood and then carve to this line using the No. 3/30, tapering the angle from the back down to the front.

Sanding

22 Sand your sculpture through all of the grits, using the hot-water technique in between each one (see page 63). Cut it off the base and sand the bottom edges.

Finishing

The finish used for the Female Torso on page 123 was two coats of clear wax polish, which sealed the wood and gave it a wonderful sheen on the surface.

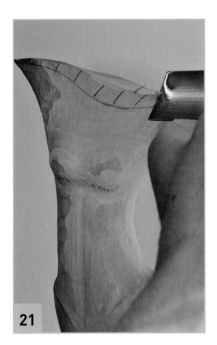

21

Base

(See **A**, **B**, **C** and **D**.) The base is made from a piece of American black walnut, measuring H ⅝ x W 2¾ x D 4in (16 x 70 x 102mm) before cutting. Use the template provided on page 124 to transfer the design onto your wood. Cut it out directly around the outer edge of the line.

Measure 1⅜in (35mm) from the front and back positions of the wood in towards the center and mark these positions with a bradawl. Drill two ³⁄₁₆in (4mm or 5mm) holes in these positions and then countersink them from the underside.

Now sand the base through all the grits, using the hot-water technique in between each one. Finally, if you wish to achieve the same finished effect as the example shown on page 123, apply a thin layer of boiled linseed oil, followed one week later by two applications of a dark wax polish.

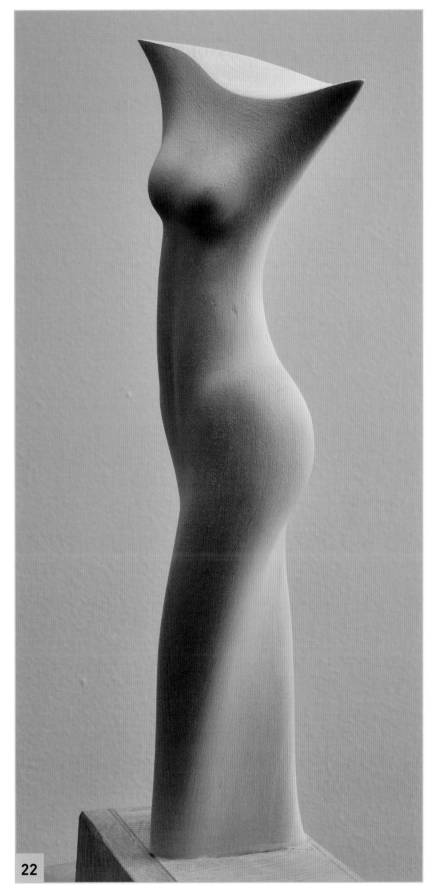

22

SWAN

Difficulty level: 6/10 on the
beginner's scale

Time to complete:
25–40 hours

THIS DESIGN IS AN ELEGANT ABSTRACTION OF A SWAN,
DEPICTING THE REAL ESSENCE OF THIS BEAUTIFUL CREATURE
WITH ITS SLENDER, FLUID LINES OF THE WING OVER THE BODY
AND GENTLE CURVED NECK, BRINGING MOVEMENT AND LIFE
TO THIS MAJESTIC BIRD.

The design of this project can be modified in many different areas so
that you can incorporate your own ideas – for example, the body does
not have to be pierced through the middle; it could be one solid piece,
which would make the exercise slightly easier but put the emphasis on
you to solve any arising issues. The angles of the wings can be adjusted
to reflect how you would like to portray them, and the curves flowing
from the body, through the neck and head, can also be modified to suit
your preference and vision.

The curved angles of the body and head are simple in form but quite
complex to execute, as you will have to keep changing your angle of
approach to the grain each time the angle of the design changes direction,
especially through the head and neck. The angles here not only flow
from left to right but also from front to back, requiring you to change the
direction of your cut many times. This will test you somewhat but give you
a great exercise in understanding grain direction and how to approach it.

What you will learn

- How and where to adapt the design to your
  personal vision
- How to remove large quantities of wood with
  a coping saw
- How to approach difficult grain directions
- Basic knife work
- How to separate different levels of detail
- How to give the illusion of different volumes
- How to make a base and mount the sculpture

TOOLS

No. 2/20
No. 3/30
No. 5/20
No. 7/20
No. 9/10
No. 12/10
Knife (new for this project)
Drill bit – 5/32in (4mm)
Brad-point drill bit
Coping saw (optional)

WOOD

Lime (basswood)

Dimensions before cutting
profile: H 10 x W 12 x D 5in
(254 x 305 x 127mm)

Dimensions of Swan: H 8 x W 11¼
x D 4½in (203 x 286 x 115mm)

Lime wood was chosen for this
project for its appropriate light
color which lends itself to the
subject beautifully. It can be
bleached to produce an almost
pure white finish.

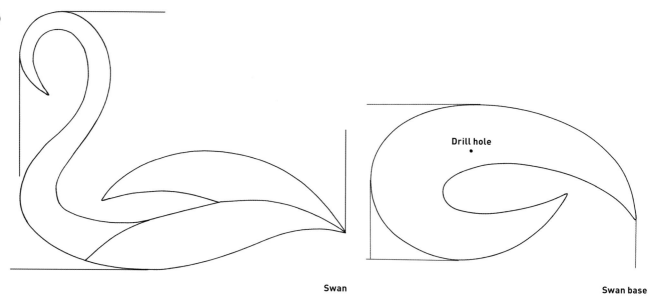

Swan

Drill hole

Swan base

SCALE DESIGN AND CUTTING OUT

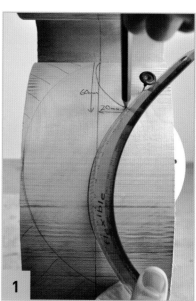

Due to the design of the Swan, it is only possible to cut the side profile; the rest will have to be carved by hand as you feel your way into the project.

Enlarge the scale drawing and apply it to your prepared block of wood – making sure that the grain of your block is running horizontally through the design – and cut it out as described on pages 78–81.

Mount the sawn form onto your vise and mark the center line all the way around the wood.

THE CARVING

Before you start working on the piece, read through the step guide to see how the form develops and study pictures **A**–**E** to familiarize yourself with the finished form that you are aiming to produce.

The upper wing

1 (See **E**.) Using your flexible rule, draw the shape of the upper wing onto your wood, using the complete length of this upper section. Here, the top edge of the wing started at the position of the center line, came down 2⅜in (60mm) and then finished ¾in (20mm) to the right of the center line. You can make yours the same shape as here, or adapt it to your own design.

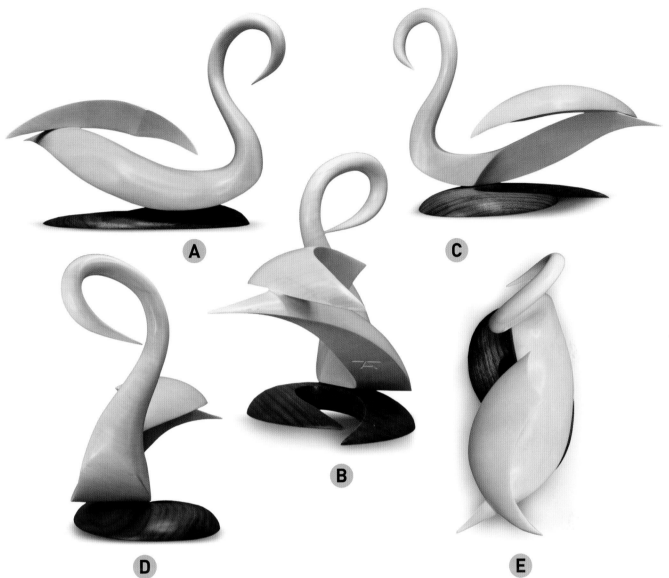

A

C

B

D

E

TIP If you don't have a willing helper to assist you in holding the rule, use a thumbtack, as shown in picture **1**, to hold the flexible rule in position while you mark the curve of the wing onto your wood.

2 (See **C** and **E**.) Use your No. 3/30 or No. 5/20 to pare the wood back to the line on the left-hand front edge of the wing.

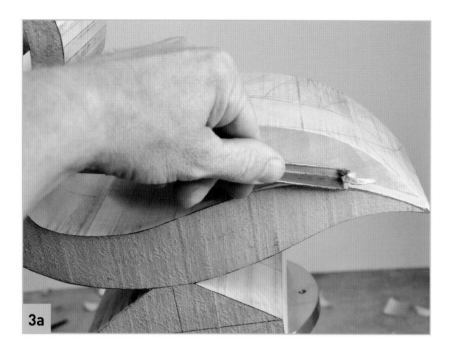

3a

3b

3 (See **C** and **E**.) Use the No. 12/10 V-Tool with the shoulder flat on the line, working inwards along the line of the body **3a**. Then use the No. 3/30 to pare the wood back to the depth of the V-Tool cut. Repeat this procedure until you have pared the wood back to the design line of the upper wing **3b**.

4 (See **A** and **E**.) Now turning to the opposite side, use the No. 5/20 to pare the wood back to the design line at the top edge of the wing.

5 (See **A** and **E**.) Because of the inner curvature on this side of the wing, you will need to remove the surplus wood working across the grain. Do this using the No. 7/20 down to the line of the body – use the template for reference. Don't worry about getting the edge cut right back square to the line at this stage, as you will be going back to this area in steps 18 and 19.

4

5

6a

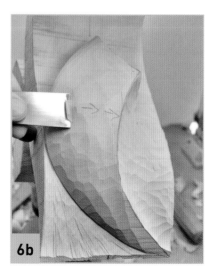

6b

7

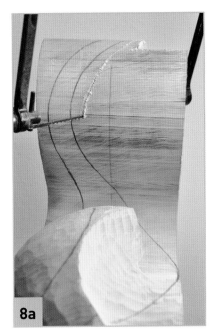

8a

8b

9a

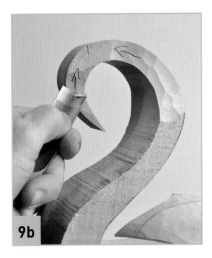

9b

6 (See **B**, **C** and **E**.) The upper wing is naturally curved from the top of the right edge down to the bottom of the left edge. Carve this following the directions you can see marked on the wood in **6a** and **6b** using the No. 3/30.

Head and neck

7 (See **A**, **B**, **C**, **D** and **E**.) Study pictures A–E to help you understand the angles you are trying to produce and then draw the basic shape of the head and neck onto the wood. As you can see in the picture, the lower part of the body as well as the neck and head have been drawn onto the wood. This helps to give an understanding of the balance and flow of the design – a very important element of this sculpture. Do the same with your wood and either copy the design shown here or adapt it to your own version.

8 (See **B** and **D**.) There is quite a lot of wood to cut away from either side of the head and neck, so it is logical to do this as effectively as possible with a coping saw. Make sure that you brace the wood firmly with your spare hand and don't put too much pressure into the sawing movements **8a**, **8b**.

9 (See **A**, **B**, **C**, **D** and **E**.) You can now use your No. 5/20 to pare the wood back to the line on both sides of the head and neck, following the directions of cut illustrated in **9a** and **9b**.

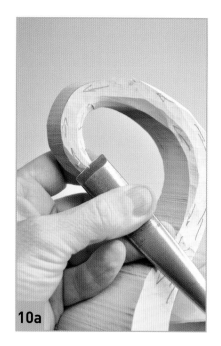

10a

10b

11

10 (See **A**, **B**, **C**, **D** and **E**.) We now come to the tricky part of the head and neck – the rounding of the edges. These do not have to be completely rounded over with the gouge, as you can use the 100-grit to finish shaping them later.

The directions of cut have been drawn on the wood in pictures **10a** and **10b** for you to follow. Remember to make very shallow cuts, and as soon as you feel any resistance in the grain, stop and change direction. You will also have to make sure that you carefully brace the opposite side of the wood with your fingers, as demonstrated in **10a**. Use your No. 5/20 upside down so that the curvature of the sweep is lending itself to the curved angle that you are trying to create, and carve your way around the complete surface.

11 Your carving should now look like this.

12 Sand over the entire area with 100-grit to finish rounding over the edges and bring the detail to life.

Lower body

13 (See **C** and **E**.) Turn your attention to the lower part of the body. This edge of the wood has to be pared back underneath the upper wing to meet the design line of the body and neck that you drew earlier in step 7. Use your V-Tool to cut along the line of the body **13a**, and your No. 5/20 to pare the wood back underneath the upper wing, working from both directions in towards the center and then up across the grain in the center of the body's curve **13b**.

14 (See **C**.) As you work your way across underneath the wing you will reach the point when you need to cut the base back below the body for easier access to this area. This will require you to move the sculpture

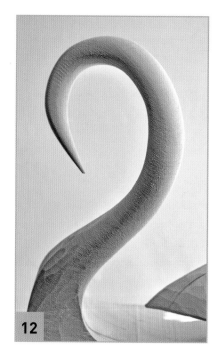

12

over the edge of your faceplate so that you can undercut this successfully. Do this with the No. 7/20 and then continue carving the body back until you reach the design line of the body.

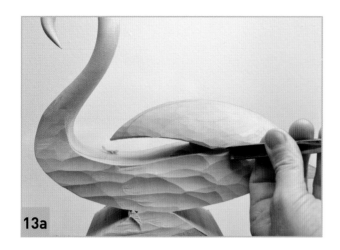

13a

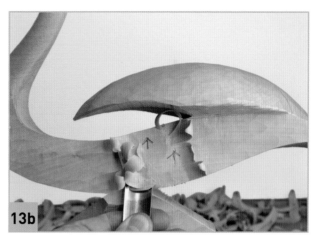

13b

14

15a

15 (See **B**, **C** and **D**.) The final job to do on this lower part of the body is to undercut a section of it below the upper wing. On the design shown here, the natural curvature of the body has been extended down on the left side to mirror the angle of the tail on the right. The body measures 8¼in (210mm) from the tip of the tail to this position **15a**. Draw this curve onto your wood then pare away the wood underneath the upper line of the body back to an undercut of about ¾in (20mm) in the center, gradually tapering out in both directions **15b**. You may find it necessary to cut the base back even further to give you enough access to carve this depth.

15b

16

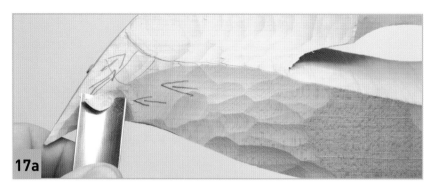

17a

17b

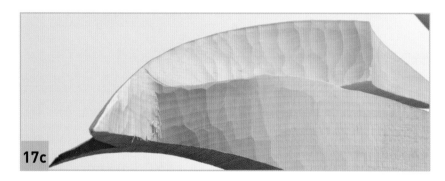

17c

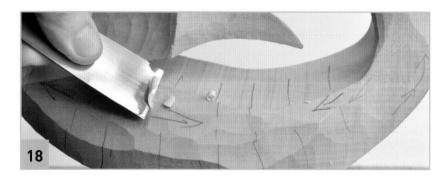

18

Separating the tail feathers

16 (See **B** and **E**.) You have now reached the most technically challenging area of the carving: the separation of the tail feathers. The first task is to remove the hatched area between the two tail ends carefully. This is accomplished by using the No. 2/20, working along both inner edges of the tail until they meet at an angle in the middle.

17 (See **A** and **E**.) Next, carve the excess wood back to the design lines of the body and the adjoining upper wing. Use the No. 7/20 and the No. 9/10 to cut along the tip and edge of the upper wing **17a** and the No. 5/20 to pare the body back in towards these cuts **17b**. Repeat this procedure until you reach both lines **17c**.

18 (See **A**.) The lower body now has to be shaped so that its natural finished curvature can be extended underneath the upper wing and wingtip. Start shaping the body using the No. 3/30, curving the outer edge and working in towards the center until you reach the position where you left off in step 5.

19 (See **Ⓐ**.) Continue shaping this area by pushing the mass back in towards and underneath the upper wing. Use the V-Tool on its side to cut along the line of the upper wing **19a** and then the No. 5/20 to pare the wood back into the V-Tool cut **19b**. You can then go further by undercutting the wing to a depth of about ⅜in (10mm) in the center, gradually tapering it out towards the wingtip. This undercut can then be extended around to the very front section of the upper wing. You should now have access to continue shaping the complete surface of the body with a gentle curve from the outer edge to the inner edge, paying special attention to the contour at the position where the wingtips cross over **19c**.

20 (See **Ⓐ**.) Your sculpture should now look like this and is ready for the separation of the wingtips. You will need to approach this area with a very delicate touch and finesse of technique – make shallow cuts and do not rush the process. Draw the line of the tail onto your wood, carefully following the contour of the upper wing to produce its gentle flowing curve.

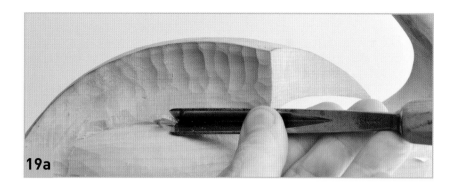

19a

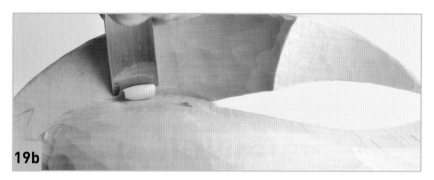

19b

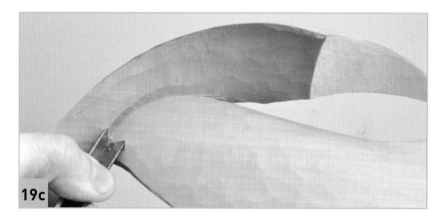

19c

20

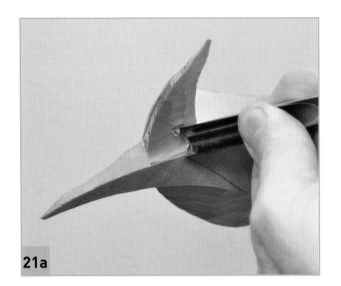

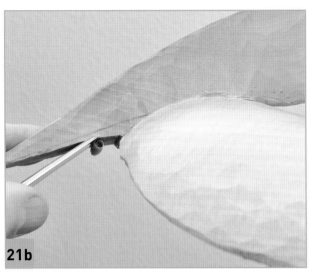

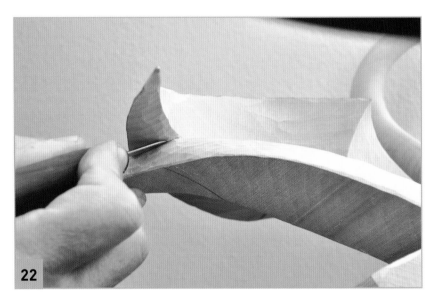

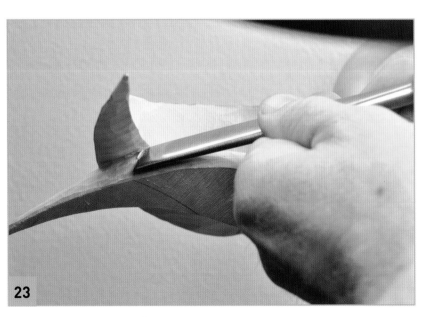

21 (See **A** and **B**.) Start by using the No. 9/10, making gentle shallow cuts to delicately remove the lower part of the hatched area underneath the top wing, following the line of the lower body **21a**. Use the No. 2/20 to pare the wood away from the underside line of the top wing, in towards the No. 9/10 cut, carefully bracing the top wing tip with your fingers, as demonstrated in **21b**.

22 (See **A** and **B**.) When you have progressed as far as you can reach in between the wings with the No. 9/10, continue with the knife by making shallow cuts using very little pressure, following the same angle as the upper wing.

23 (See **A** and **B**.) Use the No. 2/20 again to pare away the wood along the lower wing into the knife cut. Repeat steps 21–23, gradually curving the lower body and wingtip naturally underneath the upper wing.

24 (See **Ⓐ** and **Ⓑ**.) The final touches that need to be made to the upper wing and body will create the illusion that these two volumes are separate to one another. Holding the knife at a slightly inward angle, make a slice along the body at the position where the wing and body touch **24a**. Use the No. 2/20 to make a very shallow cut along the body into the knife slit **24b**. You may need to repeat these procedures to produce the desired visual effect of the wing naturally lying on top of the body.

25 (See **Ⓒ**.) We now move to the final area of carving on the sculpture, the underside of the upper wing from the position where the wing and body cross over, then forward to the front of the wing. As you can see in the picture, the contour line here should curve naturally from the angle of the wingtip up in a gradual curve and then back down to the front of the wing. Draw this line carefully onto your wood and use the No. 5/20 to pare the wood back to this line. Continue blending this contour underneath the wing to produce an even depth across the complete surface.

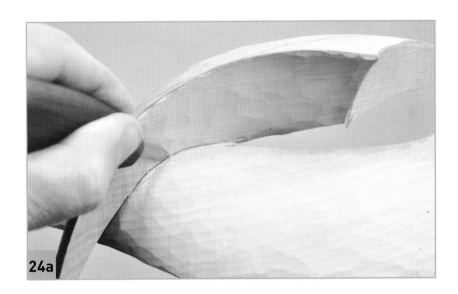

24a

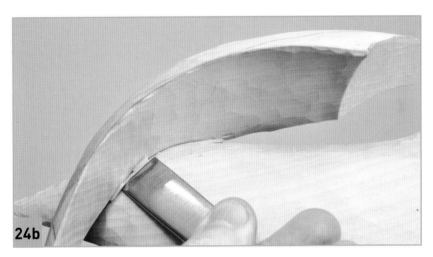

24b

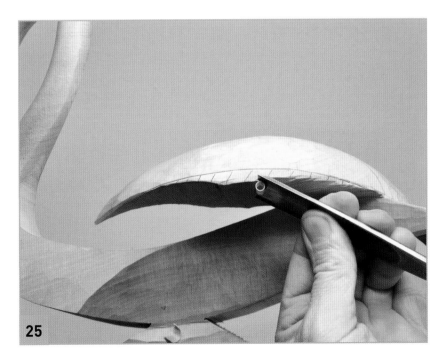

25

26

26 Your sculpture is now finished and should look like this.

Sanding
Sand your swan through all the grits, using the hot-water technique in between each one (see page 63), then cut it off at the base and sand the bottom edges.

Finishing
The completed example of the Swan on page 135 was finished with three coats of a two-part wood bleach to give a very light, white, almost porcelain effect, which is appropriate for the subject and a very beautiful finish with the grain delicately showing through the patina. When this procedure was completed, the surface was rubbed over with a 1,200-grit cloth before applying two coats of clear wax polish to produce a very fine finish. You can do the same, or use another finish of your preference.

Base
The design for the base is an almost reflective shadow of the lower body and tail with a very sleek contour flowing from the front to the back. It is not the same length as the swan, as this would not give a good balance to the sculpture, but rather sits back in underneath the body, adding an even greater visual impact to the fluid, sleek lines of the complete design. It is made from a block of American black walnut with an original size before cutting of H 3¾ x W 8½ x D 4½ in (20 x 215 x 115mm). It was finished with linseed oil and dark wax.

A template is provided on page 136 to help you produce your base, but this will need to be adapted slightly to follow the body line of your own swan.

27

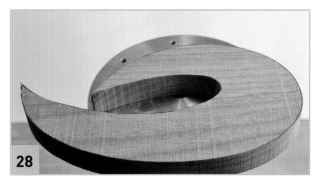

28

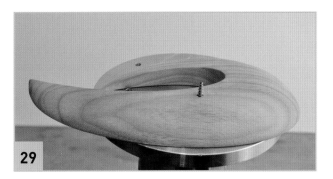

29

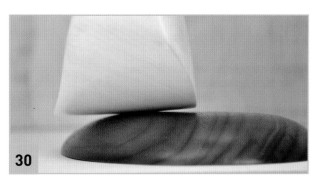

30

27 (See **A**, **B** and **C**.) To produce the correct contour for your own sculpture, you simply have to hold it in position on the template with the undercut of the body at the front of the inner curve of the base. You will then have to sight in the angle of the body as it flows back towards the tail and draw this onto the template. It doesn't need to be exact, but do make sure that the first inch or so (20–25mm) of the body that will be touching the base corresponds with its shape. The opposite side of the curve on the base does not need any alterations, as this is not meant to be reflecting anything.

28 When you are quite sure that you have the correct angles in the right places, transfer the design onto your wood, cut it out and mount it on your vise.

29 (See **A**, **B**, **C** and **D**.) The highest position of the base is at the front edge of the inner curve (see **27** and **29**). From this position, the front edge and both of the rear tips are to be evenly tapered down and rounded over to the outer edge. The curvature of the front edge then needs to be evenly extended all of the way around both sides of the design, leaving the inner vertical edge flat and uncarved. This is all accomplished by using the No. 3/30.

30 To attach your swan in position on its base, the base will first need to be drilled with a ⁵⁄₃₂in (4mm) brad-point drill bit and then countersunk from underneath for the screw head to sit flush in the wood. The position for the drill hole has been marked on the template provided, but please be aware

that you may need to adjust this position to suit your individual base. The actual positional measurements of the drill hole in the example shown here are 3¼in (83mm) back from the front edge and ½in (13mm) in from the inner curve.

When you have created your drill hole, hold the sculpture in position with the undercut of the body in line with the inner curve (see **27**), making sure that it is level and not leaning over either side, and then screw the two parts securely together. Lastly, remove the sculpture from the base again, sand the base through all of the grits using the hot-water technique in between each one and finish it with a wood preparation of your choice.

EMPEROR PENGUIN

Difficulty level: 7/10 on the beginner's scale

Time to complete: 30–50 hours

THE EMPEROR PENGUIN IS THE FIRST OF TWO REAL-LIFE STUDIES IN THIS BOOK. YOU WILL BE UTILIZING MANY OF THE TECHNIQUES THAT YOU HAVE ALREADY LEARNED IN PREVIOUS PROJECTS ALONG WITH SOME NEW ONES TO HELP YOU TO PRODUCE A CONVINCING REPLICATION OF THIS WONDERFUL CREATURE.

This is a gentle introduction to real-life studies and fairly simple to produce. It has just three main detailed areas to study: the head, wings and feet. These involve some delicate gouge and knife work, which will help you to develop finesse in your technique – finesse being an essential instrument in three-dimensional work.

You can never have too much reference material at your disposal, and when studying real-life subjects, it is of the utmost importance to understand visually exactly what you are trying to reproduce before you make any attempt to apply the detail. There is an abundance of appropriate Internet resources for your reference. Make sure that you are searching the image and/or video section of the search engine and use such search terms (in double quotes) as "emperor penguin head," "emperor penguin feet," "emperor penguin tail" and so on.

American black walnut was chosen for its strength, color and suitability for the subject. The details of the bill, wings and feet are fragile, so it was important to use a stronger wood less likely to snap. The lighter sapwood was positioned on the front side of the penguin where it would be white in real life, helping to bring realism to the subject.

What you will learn

- How to carve with delicacy and finesse
- How to carve the detail of the bill
- How to carve the detail of the eye
- How to carve the detail of the fins
- How to carve the detail of the tail
- How to carve the detail of the feet
- Advanced knife work

TOOLS

No. 1S/5 (new for this project – optional)
No. 2/5 (new for this project)
No. 2/12 (new for this project)
No. 3/20 (new for this project)
No. 3/30
No. 5/20
No. 7/6
No. 7/20
No. 8/7 (new for this project)
No. 9/10
No. 12/3 (new for this project)
No. 12/10
Knife
Round riffler file (optional)
Bradawl
Drill bit – ½in (13mm)
Brad-point drill bit
Drill bit – ⅛in (2–3mm)
Brad-point drill bit

WOOD

American black walnut

Dimensions before cutting profiles: H 9½ x W 5 x D 4in (240 x 130 x 100mm)

Dimensions of Penguin: H 8¼ x W 4⅜ x D 3⅞in (210 x 111 x 98mm)

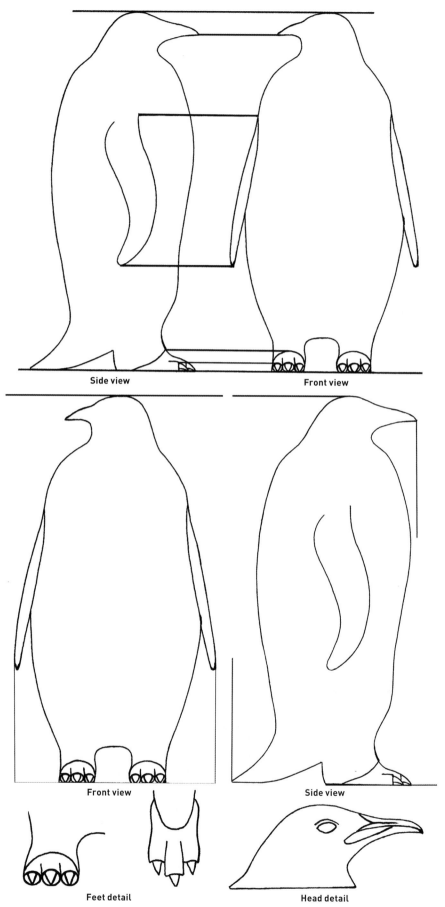

Side view

Front view

Front view

Side view

Feet detail

Head detail

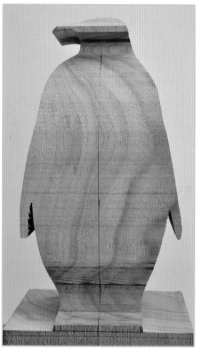

SCALE DESIGN
AND CUTTING OUT

Enlarge the front and side scale
drawings provided to the correct
size, apply them to your prepared
block of wood – making sure that
the grain of your block is running
vertically through the design –
then cut both profiles out (see
pages 78–81). Mount the sawn
form onto your vise and mark the
center line all the way around the
front and back of the wood.

A   B   C   D

E   1

THE CARVING

Before you start working on the piece, read through the step guide to see how the form develops and study pictures **A**–**E** above to familiarize yourself with the finished form that you are aiming to produce.

Head

1 (See **E**.) The order of work on this subject is to start at the head, then work down through the body and finish with the feet. Your first job is to remove the bandsaw extensions either side of the bill, placing it roughly in position with the head turned to the right. Study pictures **1** and **E** above to give you an understanding of this angle and then carve it in position with the No. 2/12.

2a

2b

3

2 (See **A**, **B**, **C**, **D** and **E**.) Round over the square edges of the head, working around the shoulders and chest, up under the bill and over the back of the head. The No. 3/20 is used to remove the square edges and blend the areas of the head evenly together **2a**. The No. 9/10 is used to curve the areas around the neck line underneath the bill **2b**.

3 (See **E**.) The bill can now be placed in its precise position. Measure and mark the center position of the head onto your wood and draw a center line from the tip of the bill to the back of the head. Measure 1in (25mm) back from the tip of the bill and mark this position on the center line. Measure out ³⁄₁₆in (5mm) from this position on both sides of the center line and mark. Connect these two positions to the tip of the bill then taper the line naturally back onto the head. Use the No. 2/12 to pare the wood back to these lines.

4 (See **A**, **B** and **D**.) The line where the bill opens runs centrally along the bill's length to the inner corner near the eye where it curves down slightly. The length of this line is approximately 1³⁄₁₆in (30mm) from the tip to the inner corner. Using the drawing of the head supplied as a reference, measure and draw this line carefully onto both sides of the bill and check for correct alignment from the front view. Use the No. 2/12 to gently pare away the wood at an angle, either side of the line up onto the top of the bill and down underneath it, which will produce the widest point at the position where the bill opens. As you work towards the tip of the bill, make sure you brace the wood with your finger on the opposite side to help prevent it snapping along the grain.

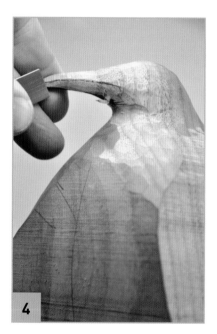

4

When you have shaped both sides of the bill, use a piece of 100-grit sandpaper to sand over the head and bill completely. Check that both sides of the head and bill are symmetrical and make any necessary adjustments.

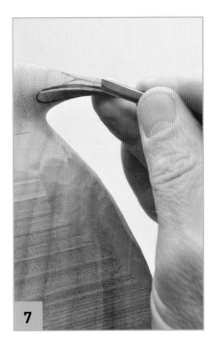

5 At this stage it is particularly important to gather as much reference material as you can find to help you to understand and apply the details of the bill onto your wood. Emperor penguins have a rather complex and elaborate bill, with a bright orange patch on the side of the mouth opening and grooves along its length. Study these details carefully and use the head drawing supplied as a reference to help you transfer these details symmetrically onto both sides of your wood.

6 (See **B** and **D**.) Before you try to cut the opening line of the bill, it is very important to give your knife a quick strop to ensure that it is razor sharp – ten strokes a side should be ample. This should be repeated after every cut to keep the edge keen and minimize the chance of it slipping.

Start at the tip of the bill, using almost no pressure whatsoever. Gently rub the edge of the blade back and forth along the line to slowly create a shallow dividing cut, then, as you work back along the length of the bill, add more and more pressure to produce a deeper cut.

7 (See **B** and **D**.) To produce the dividing line of the bill, use the No. 2/5 to pare back the wood delicately from the very edge next to the knife cut into the knife cut. Repeat steps 6 and 7 again to reach the correct depth to produce the realistic effect of the bill. The tip only needs to be a fraction of an inch/millimeter deep to give the right effect.

8 (See **B** and **D**.) The other markings on the bill only require a small V-Tool and some clever shaping with sandpaper to produce the detail that we are

after. The V-Tool should be well stropped before use to minimize the risk of it slipping. Use a No. 12/3 V-Tool to sketch carefully along the lines, on and around the bill, and then a folded piece of 240-grit sandpaper to blend the V-cut and knife cuts naturally into their surrounding areas.

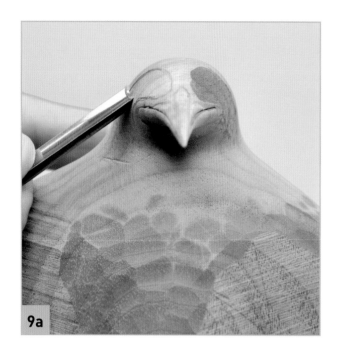

9a

9b

Eyes

9 (See **A**, **B**, **C**, **D** and **E**.)
Moving onto the eyes, study some close-up images of an emperor penguin's head and observe the slightly concave hollow where the eyes are located. This area has to be prepared before you cut the eyes into the head so that they sit at the correct angle on the side of the head when they have been carved.

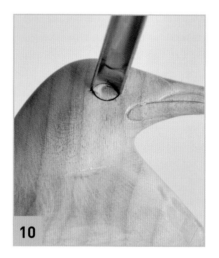

10

11

The position of the eye is about ⅛in (2–3mm) behind the corner of the mouth with the bottom curve of the eye at about the same level as the mouth. Draw the area demonstrated in pictures **9a** and **9b** accurately onto both sides of the head and use the No. 7/6 to create this hollow **9a**. Blend the depths evenly from this hollow into the surrounding areas **9b**. Check from several angles to ensure that both sides are precisely symmetrical and then sand over with 100-grit.

10 (See **A**, **B**, **C**, **D** and **E**.)
You will be using a No. 8/7 to create the shape of the eye, so you only need to measure and mark the level positions of both corners of the eye where the gouge will be placed. You can, of course, draw the eyes in position if you wish to – this may also help you to determine the precise symmetry on both sides of the head.

Using the head drawing as a reference, measure ⅛in (2–3mm) back from the corner of the

mouth and mark a vertical line in this position. Measure back a further ⁹⁄₃₂in (7mm) from this line and mark another line in this position.

Important! The following procedure must be made with the gouge at a right angle to the wood and not with the gouge leaning back at an angle, otherwise the eyeball will chip out without warning!

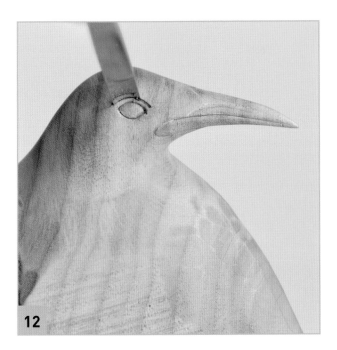

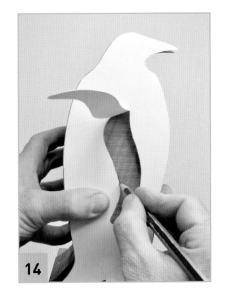

Place the No. 8/7 between these lines, with the lower edge of the gouge in line with the mouth, press it firmly into the wood and rock it from side to side. Repeat this process on the top half of the eye, joining the two halves together at each corner.

11 (See **A**, **B**, **C**, **D** and **E**.) Use the corner edge of the No. 2/5 to pare the wood back from the surface of the eye into the gouge cuts to produce the convex curve across the eye. Repeat stages 10 and 11 again if necessary, but do not attempt to make the eyeballs too spherical as they appear quite flat in real life.

12 (See **A**, **B**, **C**, **D** and **E**.) The upper eyelid can now be cut just a fraction above the eye. Use the No. 7/6, repeating the same process as for the eye, pressing firmly into the wood and rocking it gently from side to side. Then use the No. 2/5 to

pare the wood back into this cut. The final job is to sand gently over the eyes and eyelids with 240-grit. Fold your sandpaper to produce a pointed tip (see page 65) and smooth over all of the details, blending them naturally together.

13 Your carving should now look like this, which means that you have successfully completed the head.

Wings

14 (See **B** and **D**.) Now move onto the wings. Carefully cut around the shape of the wing on your template, hold it in position on your carving and draw it onto the wood. Repeat this on the opposite side and check for symmetry.

15 (See **B** and **D**.) Sketch around the very outer line of the wing with the No. 12/10 V-Tool.

16 (See **A**, **B**, **C** and **D**.) Use the No. 3/20 to pare away the wood to the depth of the No. 12 cut. Repeat steps 15 and 16 until you reach the correct depth of approximately ¼in (6–7mm) at the position where the wings rest on the body, tapering down flush as you reach the upper end adjacent to the chest.

17 (See **A**, **B**, **C**, and **D**.) The wings have a shallow curve across their width, which needs to be delicately shaped with the No. 2/12. Carefully pare away a little of the depth from both outer edges of the wings, blending them evenly up onto the center to produce this slight curve. This detail can then be sanded with 100-grit to check how realistic the wings appear and further worked if necessary.

18 (See **A**, **B**, **C**, and **D**.) To add to the realism of the wings you need to produce an undercut along their edges to give the impression that they are just resting on the surface of the body. This effect is achieved by making an inward knife cut at the position where the wing is resting on the surface of the body **18a** and then paring the wood away along the body into the knife cut with the No. 2/12 **18b**. This is repeated until the wing appears to be separate from the body with shadow between the two details. Finally, the edges can be sanded into these cuts to complete their realistic effect.

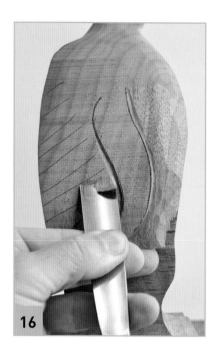

16

17

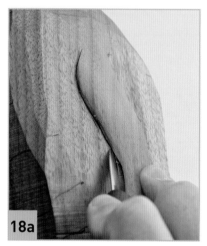

18a

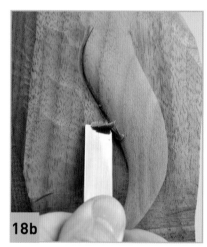

18b

Body

19 (See **A**, **B**, **C**, **D** and **E**.) The body of the penguin is fairly simple to shape, as you have already established the exact front and side profiles when you first cut it out. But care must be taken to ensure that you remove enough wood to eliminate any square-looking edges.

Study your reference material to see how the natural contour of the body is formed. Use the No. 3/30, working from the four

19

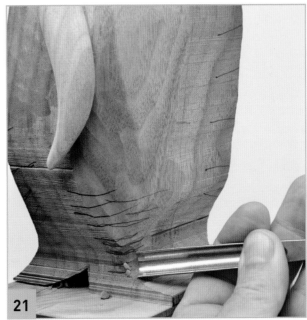

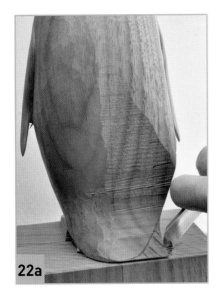

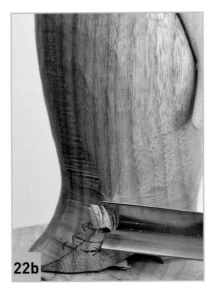

square corners, in a natural curve around onto the center line of the chest, back and sides, progressing evenly down the length of the body.

20 A tip to bear in mind when you are creating symmetrical curves, such as the penguin's body, is that it is very helpful to draw a line from one side to the other. By doing this, you will gain a clearer

visual understanding of how symmetrical the contour of the surface actually is.

21 (See **A**, **B** and **D**.) Moving down the body now to the area just above the feet, use the No. 9/10 to pare away the wood around this lower edge in a natural curve from the front around to the side. Use the No. 5/20 to blend the depths into their surrounding areas.

22 (See **B**, **C** and **D**.) We shall look at the tail in detail next but before that, use the No. 3/20 to remove its lower square edges, curving them around from the side of the body to the tip **22a**. Then use the No. 7/20 to blend the mass from the square lower edge up onto the center of the tail **22b**. Finally, use the No. 3/30 to finish off curving the lower part of the body evenly into the tail area **22c**.

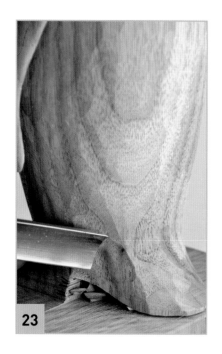

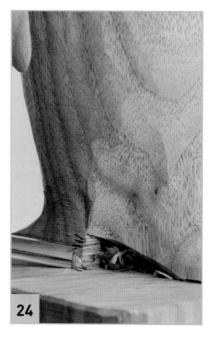

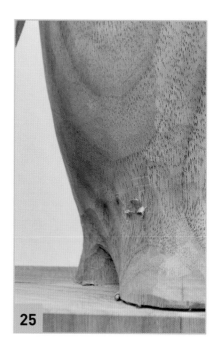

Tail

23 (See **B**, **C** and **D**.) Moving straight onto the detail of the tail now, the first job you must do is to carve it to its correct shape and size. Study your reference material and pictures **C** and **26** to gain an understanding of the shape that you are trying to create. Starting on the left side, use the No. 7/20 again, working directly around the back of the legs, carving this area approximately ⅜in (10mm) inwards from the edge and curving it naturally back towards the rear tip of the tail, then blend in the adjoining areas of the lower back.

24 (See **B**, **C** and **D**.) The rear of the leg on this side can now also be curved around naturally underneath the tail. Do this with the No. 7/6.

25 (See **B**, **C** and **D**.) The left side is complete and ready to be sanded. Repeat steps 23 and 24 on the opposite side and then sand the entire area with 100-grit.

26 (See **B**, **C** and **D**.) An emperor penguin's tail feathers are very fine in appearance but seem to vary between individuals. For this project, we shall keep it simple and just carve them around the edge of the tail.

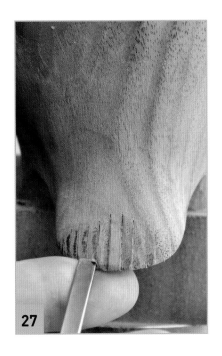

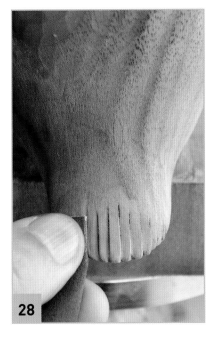

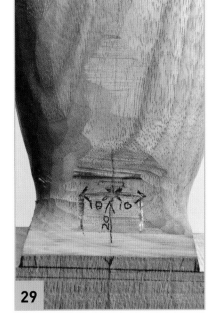

Start at the center of the tail and make the first feather you work on the middle feather. Measure out from both sides of this middle one and draw each feather about ⅛in (2–3mm) apart, becoming slightly narrower as you get near the sides of the tail. Using the knife, cut carefully along these lines, lightening the pressure of the cut as you work towards the tip of the feathers, and stop before the knife slips off the edge. Now, simply reverse the cut by pushing the blade away from you over the detail line but using the length of the blade to make the cut rather than the tip.

27 (See **B**, **C** and **D**.) To create the illusion of the feathers overlapping, you have to carefully carve just the inner edge of each feather to a depth of about ¹⁄₃₂in (0.5–1mm). The initial center feather will remain uncut in the highest position. To clarify: the feathers to the left of the center feather should be carved

just on the right of each edge, and the feathers to the right of the center feather should be carved just on the left of each edge, producing the appearance that they are overlapping each other.

Use the No. 2/5 for this job, carefully using the edge of the chisel to pare away delicately the edge of the feather into the knife cut. Be careful not to try to cut any deeper with the No. 2 than the depth of the knife cut, otherwise the feather will chip out. Repeat this procedure, if need be, to gain the correct depth.

28 (See **B**, **C** and **D**.) Use a piece of folded 150-grit to smooth and shape the feathers and enhance the finished effect.

Feet

29 (See **A**.) Before you start work on the feet, you need to cut off the rear portion of the square base that the penguin stands on, just behind the legs. This will give you full access to the areas on which you need to work. Picture **30** on page 160 shows this removed.

Measure ¾in (20mm) up from the base of the feet and draw a horizontal line in this position. Measure ⅜in (10mm) outwards from the center line on both sides and draw vertical lines to join the horizontal one. This places the legs into their correct positions and marks the area between the legs that will be removed.

30

31

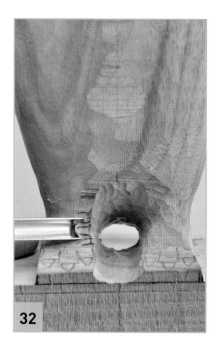

32

30 Use a ½in (13mm) brad-point drill bit to drill the hole, placed centrally on the boxed area that you measured and carefully angled to miss the tail when it pierces through between the legs.

31 (See **A**, **B** and **D**.) Before you carve the details of the feet, study your reference material to gain a clear understanding of their shape and detail. Using this and the templates of the feet as a reference, draw the feet into position on your wood. You have already established the width of the legs, which should be ¾in (20mm). The middle toe is slightly longer than the ones either side, their measurements being: side, ¼in; middle, ⁵⁄₁₆in; side, ¼in (6mm; 8mm; 6mm).

Use the No. 8/7 to pare the wood away between the feet and down to the depth of the base. Then work down the lower body, in

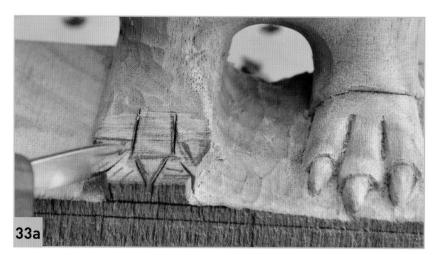

33a

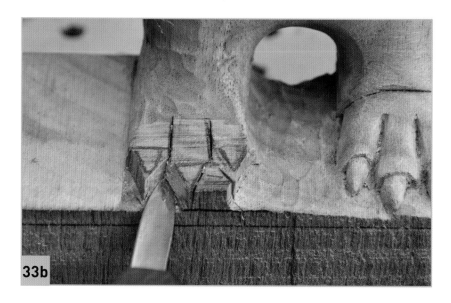

33b

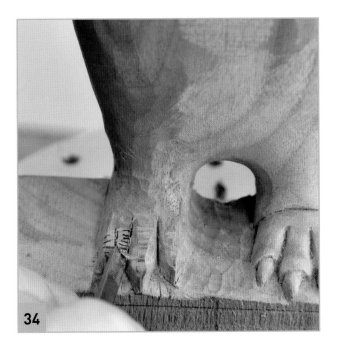

34

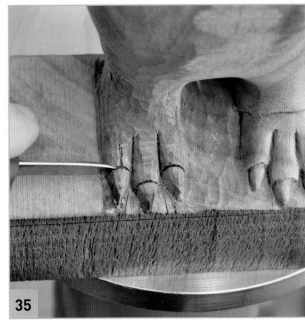

35

between the legs, opening out the drill hole into an arch shape and naturally creating a flowing line through onto the tail.

32 (See **A**, **B** and **D**.) Use the No. 8/7 to round the edges of the legs into the center hole and evenly onto the sides of the body.

33 (See **A**, **B** and **D**.) Use the knife to separate the toes and cut around the outer edges of the claws **33a**. Then, slice away the V-shaped areas of waste in between the claws, being careful not to cut deeper than your vertical cuts **33b**. Repeat these procedures until you reach the depth of the base.

34 (See **A**, **B** and **D**.) Use the No. 2/5 to round over the toes into the knife cuts to produce their natural shape. Repeat steps 33a and 34 until you achieve the realistic depth and shape of the toes.

When the penguin is cut off the base, you will have much better access to work on the detail of the claws and lower edges of the feet, so at this stage you just need to achieve the separation of the toes and the basic shape of the claws.

35 (See **A**, **B** and **D**.) A very delicate touch is needed for the details of the claws, as you will be cutting along the line of the grain, and this will snap off if you use too much pressure. It doesn't matter how many times you have to repeat this process, just take your time and you will achieve the right result.

Using the knife with very little pressure, cut along the line where the claw projects from the toes.

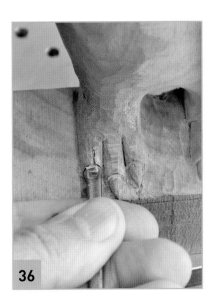

36

36 (See **A**, **B** and **D**.) Use the No. 2/5 to pare away the wood from the tips of the claws up into the knife cuts. Now repeat steps 35 and 36 until you achieve a depth of approximately $\frac{1}{32}$in (0.5–1mm). When you have reached this depth, use a piece of 100-grit sandpaper to finish shaping the curvature of the claws and the toes naturally together.

37 (See **A**, **B** and **D**.) The impression that we are trying to create here is of the feet emerging from the tight feathers on the penguin's leg. This is achieved by producing a slight variation in depth between the feathers and feet, from the inside area near the rear of the feet, going around the front of the feet, to the outside area near the rear of the feet (see side-view scale drawing).

Using the supplied scale drawings as a reference, draw the line of the feathers across the feet, from the inner to the outer areas, and check carefully for symmetry. Use the knife to cut along this line and then also to cut the horizontal line at the sole of the feet where they join the base.

38 (See **A**, **B** and **D**.) Use the No. 2/5 to pare the wood back around the feet to the depth of the knife cut **38a**. Use the No.1S/5 (or knife) to remove the waste wood in the triangular-shaped corner where the depths of the feathers and the foot are separated **38b**. Repeat steps 37 and 38 until you have achieved a depth of approximately $\frac{1}{32}$in (0.5–1mm). Sand all areas with 100-grit to blend all of the details together naturally.

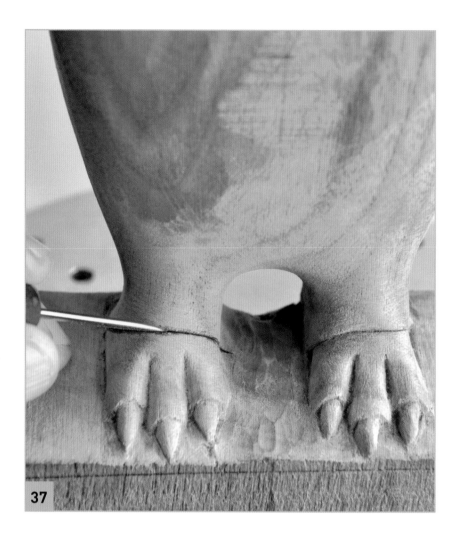

37

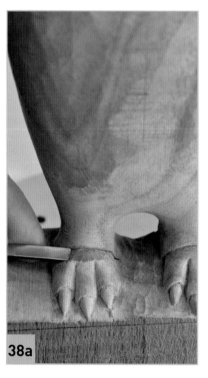

38a

38b

39

39 The final task on the feet is to curve the inner edges of the back of the legs around into the center arch. Use the No. 8/7 to do this and then sand them with 100-grit to blend the areas together.

40 Before you cut your penguin off its base to finish the feet, you must first sand it through all the grits, using the hot-water technique in between each one (see page 63). Your carving should now look like this.

Carefully cut the sculpture off its base, leaving approximately ¹⁄₃₂–¹⁄₁₆in (1–2mm) extra depth on the soles of the feet.

40

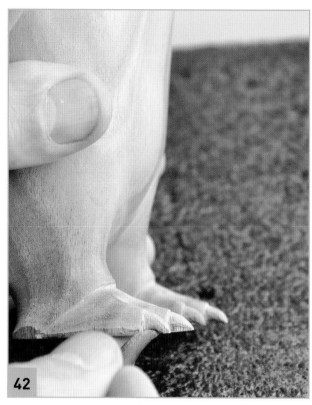

41 (See **A**, **B** and **D**.) Very carefully cut around the feet and claws with your knife, removing all of the excess wood.

42 (See **A**, **B** and **D**.) A rolled-up piece of 150-grit sandpaper or a round riffler file (a small round file used for shaping detail) can now be used to delicately produce the curve on the underside of each claw and to model it evenly to its natural shape. The same method can then also be used to round under the edges of the feet and toes. When you are satisfied that their appearance is lifelike, sand them through the remaining grits. Your sculpture is now complete.

Finishing
The finish used for the example on page 149, was firstly a thin coat of boiled linseed oil. This darkened the wood and enhanced the beauty of the grain. A dark wax polish was then applied a week later, which added a wonderful sheen to the surface and gave depth to the grain.

Base
The base is made from lime measuring H ⅞ x W 5¼ x D 4in (22 x 133 x 102mm) before cutting. The design is a simple representation of snow and ice, incorporating an asymmetrical shape with random, faceted gouge cuts around the edge to produce a balanced finish.

You can use this concept for your base if you wish, but why not have a go at designing your own to add your personal touch to the project?

43 To create a similar base to the one shown on page 149, it is advisable to secure the penguin to the base first so that you can work around its feet and tail to produce a balanced pattern of gouge cuts that work in harmony with the penguin's dimensions. To do this, place the penguin in position on your wood and draw around the feet. Next, measure and mark the central points of both legs, from the side and rear perspectives, onto your wood.

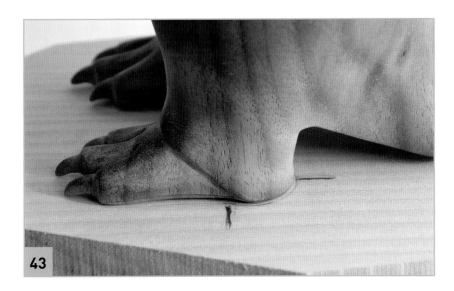

43

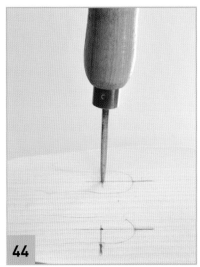

44

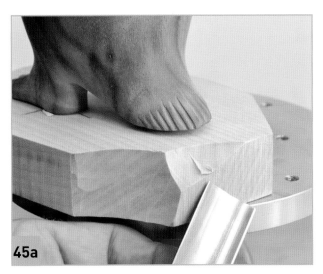

45a

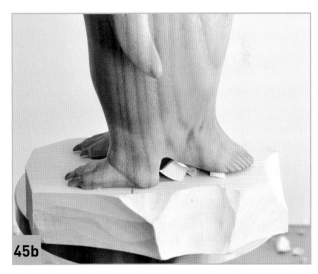

45b

44 Join these two positions together to produce the crosshairs, and mark these with a bradawl for drilling. Use a ⅛in (2–3mm) brad-point drill bit to drill the hole and then countersink it from underneath. Place your penguin accurately in position on the drilled base and carefully push the bradawl up through the holes to mark the feet. Remove from the base and make the bradawl marks deeper into the feet. Place your penguin back in position again and fix it to the base with suitably sized screws.

45 (See Ⓐ, Ⓑ, Ⓒ and Ⓓ.) Before you begin, study pictures A, B, C and D to see how the facets around the edge of the base have been formed and how they relate to the lower body, feet and tail.

To produce these facets, use the No. 7/20, to create the deeper curved gouge cuts and the No. 5/20 to create the less acute curves, working around the edges of the wood to produce adjoining random cuts and undercuts of varying degrees and depths **45a**, **45b**. Don't be afraid to experiment with the gouge cuts, but don't overwork the detail either.

Lastly, when you have finished shaping the base, you need to sand it through all of the grits, using the hot-water technique in between each one, and apply a finish of your choice. Three applications of a two-part wood bleach and clear wax polish were used to finish the example shown on page 149, which gave the lime an appropriate whitish color but still showed the grain beautifully.

HUMPBACK WHALE

Difficulty level: 9/10 on the beginner's scale

Time to complete: 60–80 hours

YOU HAVE NOW ARRIVED AT THE MOST CHALLENGING PROJECT IN THIS BOOK: A REALISTIC STUDY OF A HUMPBACK WHALE, DESIGNED TO PORTRAY ITS NATURAL, GRACEFUL MOVEMENT AND ITS UNIQUE ANATOMICAL DETAIL.

This sculpture will be accomplished by employing techniques that you have already learned in previous chapters and building on them with some interesting new ones, including adding the pectoral fins on the side of the body and the tubercles (bumps) on the head, carving the delicate detail of the flukes and pinning the whale securely to the mount. These techniques should certainly stimulate your design and problem-solving faculties and they will be invaluable to you as you progress beyond this book, as they can be utilized in many different ways, whether it's in designing and creating increasingly complex projects or in simply knowing how to mount your work in a clever and original style.

What you will learn

- How to laminate (glue) a block onto your whale to enable you to secure it to your faceplate
- How to carve the surface anatomy
- How to carve the rostrum (upper head)
- How to carve the blow holes
- How to make templates to aid your accuracy
- How to carve the detail of the eyes
- Advanced knife work
- How to carve the line of the mouth
- How to carve with delicacy and finesse
- How to carve the detail of the flukes
- How to carve the bumpy dorsal ridge
- How to effectively create the tubercles
- How to carve the ventral pleats
- How to make the pectoral fins
- How to attach the pectoral fins to the body
- How to make the sea mount
- How to mount the humpback whale on the sea mount

TOOLS

No. 1S/5
No. 2/5
No. 3/20
No. 3/30
No. 5/20
No. 7/6
No. 7/14
No. 7/20
No. 8/4 (new for this project)
No. 8/7
No. 9/10
No. 11/3 (new for this project)
Knife
Bradawl
Note: See page 169 for additional tools and materials required.

WOOD

Whale body
American black walnut
Dimensions of Humpback
Whale: H 3 x W 13 x D 4¼in
(76 x 330 x 108mm)

Pectoral fins
American black walnut
Dimensions: 2 x H 3½ x W 2
x D 1⅝in (89 x 51 x 41mm)

Tubercles
American black walnut, English walnut, ebony and lime ³⁄₃₂in and ⅛in (2mm and 3mm) dowels

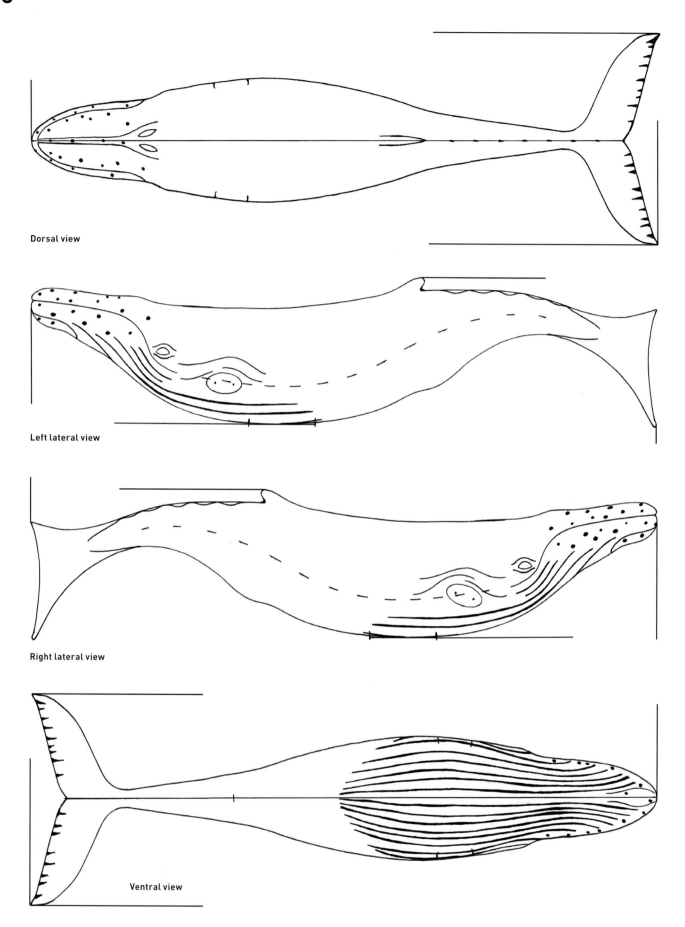

Dorsal view

Left lateral view

Right lateral view

Ventral view

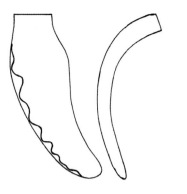

Left fin

Right fin

OTHER TOOLS AND MATERIALS

8in (20cm) length of metal pin (preferable) or wooden dowel, approximately ³⁄₃₂in (2mm or 2.4mm) in diameter, or to match the size of the drill bit that you will be using

IMPORTANT! Make sure that the grain of your block is running horizontally through the whale.

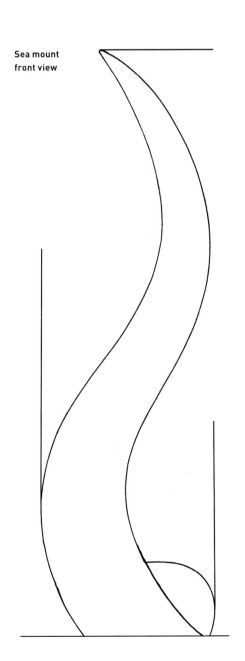

Sea mount front view

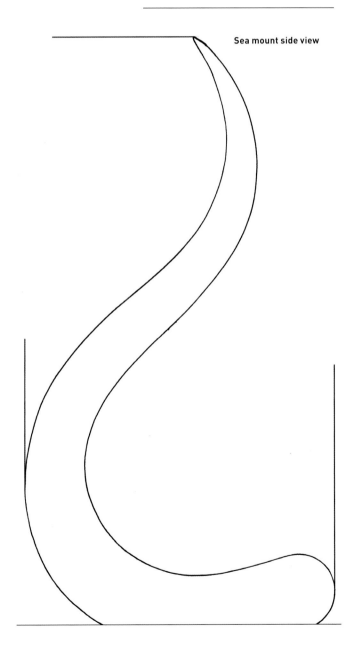

Sea mount side view

Technical consideration

The first technical matter you need to consider for this project is how to mount the whale onto the faceplate, as you won't be able to screw directly into its body. The solution to this is to glue (laminate) a separate piece of wood onto the belly area, which can then be attached to your faceplate.

SCALE DESIGN AND CUTTING OUT

1 Enlarge the scale drawings provided to the correct size for your wood. Apply the dorsal view to the top of your prepared block and the left lateral view on the left of your block, leaving a flat area of approximately 1⅜in (35mm) at the lowest area of the whale's belly, as marked on the left and right lateral views. Cut both profiles out as described on pages 78–81. Find a second piece of wood that is an appropriate size for your faceplate – or one that can be attached to another piece (as in the example in picture **3**)

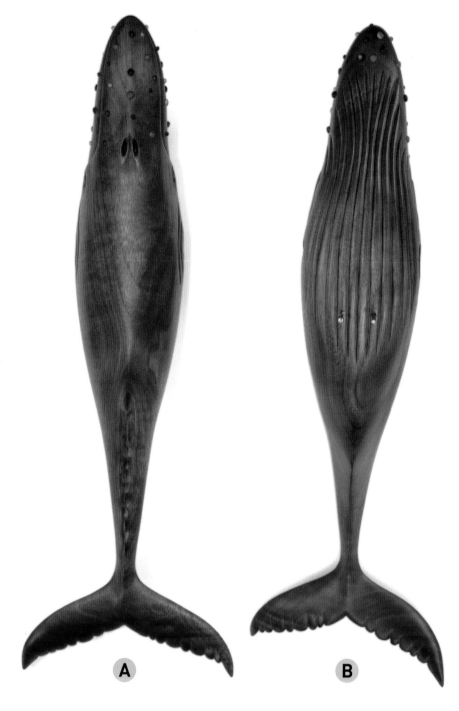

A

B

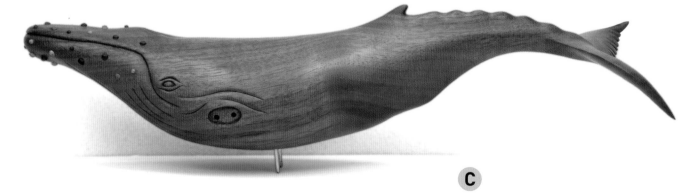

C

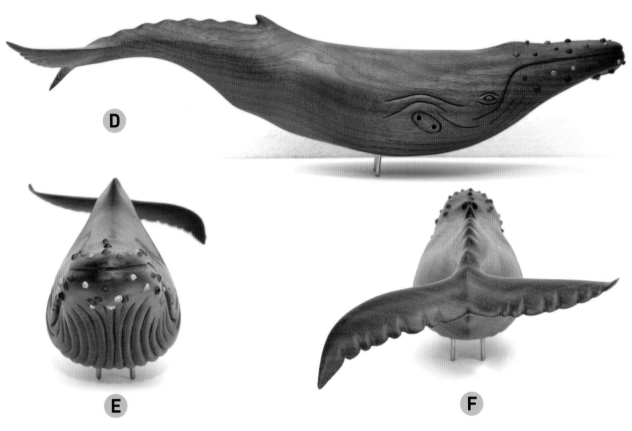

D

E

F

that will attach to the faceplate. Make sure that the surface to be bonded to the flat area of the whale is also perfectly flat. Cut the position where it will be bonded to the whale, at the exact same size as the flat area on the whale's belly, approximately 1⅜in (35mm), tapering outwards to the correct size for your faceplate. Use epoxy resin, PVA or a similar adhesive applied to both flat surfaces.

2 Carefully clamp the two pieces together, wiping off any surplus adhesive, and leave until fully dry.

3 The sawn form can now be attached securely to your vise, and a center line can be measured and marked over the top and underneath the wood.

1

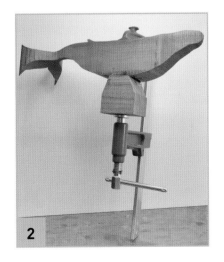

2

3

THE CARVING

Before you start working on the piece, read through the step guide to see how the form develops and study pictures **Ⓐ**–**Ⓕ** on pages 170–171 to familiarize yourself with the finished form that you are aiming to produce.

1 (See **Ⓐ**.) Using your dorsal-view scale drawing as a visual reference, measure and mark the position and shape of the whale's blow holes onto your wood.

2 (See **Ⓐ**.) Use the No. 9/10 to carve a groove around the outer edge of the blow holes' triangular shape.

3 (See **Ⓒ** and **Ⓓ**.) Using either the left or right lateral-view scale drawing as a reference, measure and mark onto your wood the widest part of the whale's body (see the dotted line on the diagrams).

4 (See **Ⓒ** and **Ⓓ**.) Use the No. 3/30 to round over the edges of the body in a natural curve, from the tip of the nose back to the dorsal fin and down to the widest part of the body.

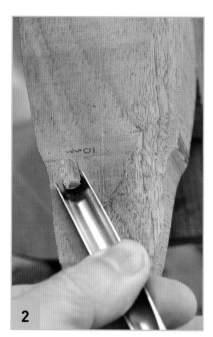

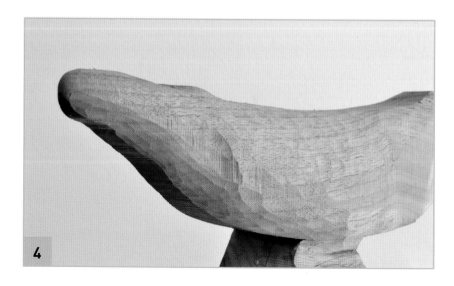

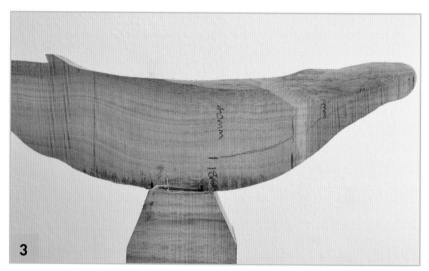

5a

5b

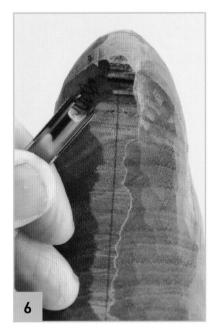

6

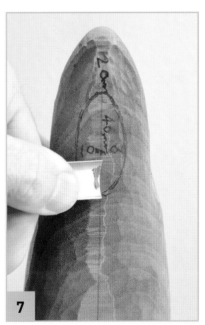

7

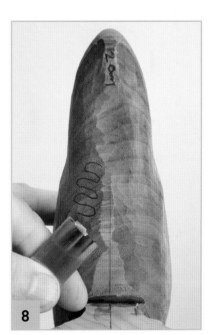

8

5 (See **B** and **E**.) In order to curve the underside of the body, you will need to pare off about ½in (13mm) from both sides of the laminated block underneath the whale. Do this using the No. 9/10 **5a**. Next, use the No. 3/20 to create a natural curve on the underside of the body, from below the mouth back to the laminated block and up to the widest point of the body **5b**. Check for symmetry on both sides and make any necessary adjustments.

6 (See **B**, **C** and **D**.) Study some images of the chin area under a humpback whale's mouth. You will see it has a sort of central bump called a chin plate, and this is normally covered in barnacles and little bumps. To produce the chin plate, use the left and right lateral-view scale drawings as references and the No. 8/7 to push the mass along the lower edge of the chin inwards towards the center from both sides until it is about ⅜in (10mm) across its width.

7 (See **B**.) Directly behind the chin plate is a slightly concave area on the underside of the mouth. To create this, draw an ellipse approximately 1½in (40mm) long by ¾in (20mm) wide. Use the No. 7/14, carving across the grain, to produce a shallow hollow in this area.

8 (See **B**.) Blend in the surrounding areas with the No. 5/20.

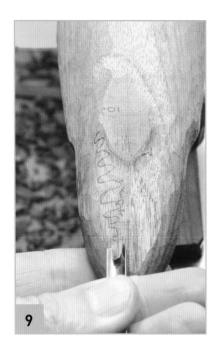

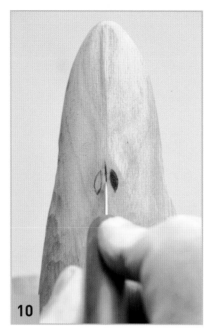

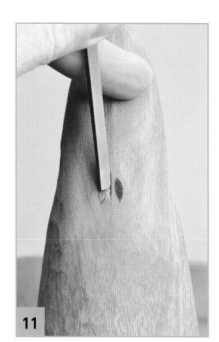

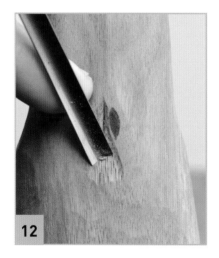

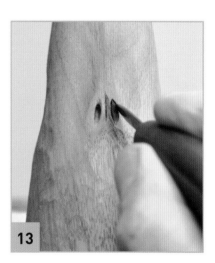

9 (See **Ⓐ**.) Study some close-up images of a humpback whale's rostrum (upper head) and see how most of this species seem to have a fairly flat area on this upper side with a ridge running along it centrally from the tip of the mouth back to the blow holes.

Use the No. 7/6 to create this ridge, working from the tip of the mouth back to the blow holes on both sides of the center line, and also to produce this flatter upper side of the rostrum. Work around the edge of the blow holes to blend in this area of depth and give more definition to the blow holes. Sand over the entire area with 100-grit.

Blow holes

10 (See **Ⓐ**.) Study some close-up images of a humpback whale's blow holes to help give you an understanding of the detail that you are trying to produce. The two holes tilt

backwards and slightly inwards, have a slit between them and a hollow at the rear.

Now use the dorsal-view scale drawing provided to transfer the correct shape and size of the blow holes onto your wood. Use the knife to slice down between them.

11 (See **Ⓐ**.) Use the No. 2/5 to pare the wood over into the knife slit.

12 (See **Ⓐ**.) Use the No. 7/6 to carve the hollow at the rear of the blow holes.

13 (See **Ⓐ**.) Use the knife, cutting at a slight inward angle, following the shape of the blow hole on both sides, so that the center of it chips out, leaving an open hole. Repeat this process to get a deeper cut inside the blow hole. Use a small piece of rolled-up 150-grit to soften the edges of the blow holes. Blend the entire area together with 100-grit.

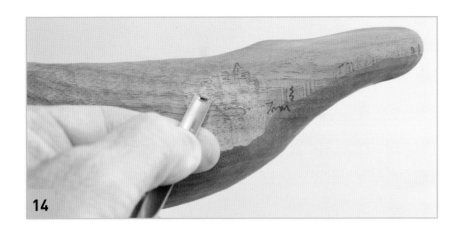

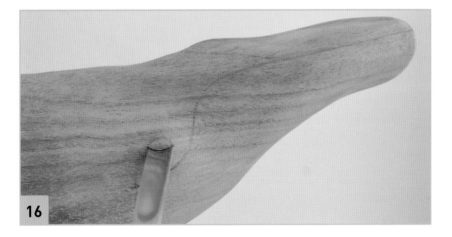

entire area with 100-grit then check for symmetry from all angles and make any necessary adjustments.

15 (See **C** and **D**.) To ensure that the eyes and mouth are precisely symmetrical on both sides of the head, it will help you to make a template of these details so that you can transfer them accurately from one side to the other. This is simply done by copying these details from one of your lateral scale drawings onto a piece of carbon paper on top of a piece of card, or, alternatively, printing your scale drawing out onto a piece of card. You can then cut around the line of the mouth with some scissors and remove the eye with the gouges that you will be using to create the eyes: a No. 7/6 along the lower edge and a No. 8/7 along the top.

Transfer these details onto both sides of your wood and check for alignment from all angles.

16 (See **C** and **D**.) Steps 16 and 17 must be performed with the gouge at a right angle to the wood, not leaning back at an angle, as this would cause the eyeball to chip out without warning.

Push the No. 7/6 firmly into the lower eyelid and rock it from side to side.

Eyes

14 (See **C** and **D**.) Study some close-up images of a humpback whale's eyes and see how they naturally bulge out from the contour of the head. Using either of your lateral-view scale drawings as a reference, measure and draw the exact positioning of the eyes onto your wood. Use the No. 7/6 to pare the wood back away from the position of the eyes, leaving them naturally raised on the surface of the head. Use the No. 3/20 to blend in the depth of the surrounding areas. Repeat on both sides. Now sand over the

17 (See **C** and **D**.) Push the No. 8/7 firmly into the upper eyelid and rock it from side to side.

18 (See **C** and **D**.) Use the No. 1S/5 or knife to slice into the corners of the eyeballs, curving them naturally into these areas.

19 (See **C** and **D**.) Use the No. 2/5 to round over the upper and lower edges of the eyeballs into the gouge cuts. Repeat steps 16 to 19 if necessary to give the impression of the spherical eyeballs.

20 (See **C** and **D**.) Using either of your lateral-view templates as a reference, draw the creases above and below the eyes onto your wood. Use the knife to cut a deep slice along the creases and the No. 2/5 to pare the wood into them. Finally, sand over the entire area of the eyes with a piece of 150-grit.

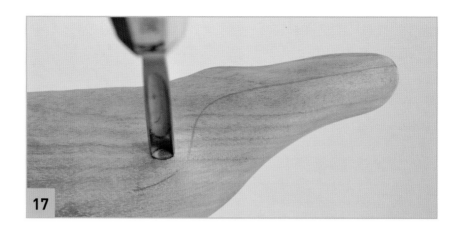

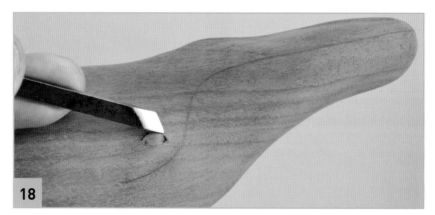

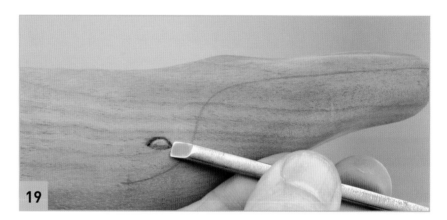

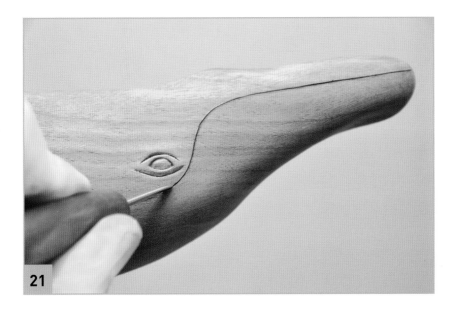

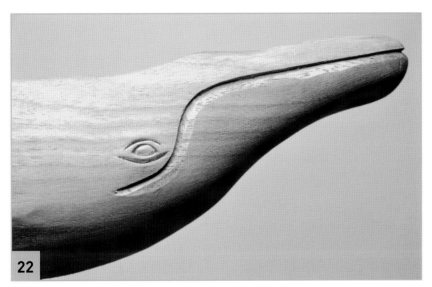

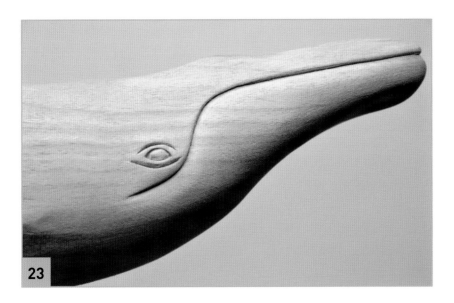

TIP Producing the detail of the mouth is a fairly simple exercise, but you must make sure that your knife is kept razor sharp by stropping it ten times on each side of the blade every time you re-cut the line – no exception.

Mouth

21 (See **C** and **D**.) Hold the knife the way that you would a pencil and draw it carefully all of the way along the line of the mouth. Make sure that you only try to make a shallow cut initially so that you produce a tram line into which you can cut deeper the second time.

22 (See **C** and **D**.) Use the No. 2/5 to pare the wood away underneath the line and into the knife cut to create the appearance of the upper jaw overhanging the lower one. Repeat steps 21 and 22 several times to produce this effect, making sure that you sharpen the knife each time.

23 Sand over the entire area with 100-grit to soften the details and blend the depths naturally together. Your sculpture should now look like this.

Body and dorsal fin

24 (See **A**, **B**, **C** and **D**.) The rear end of the whale, from the dorsal fin to the tail (the dorsal ridge), is pretty much a sharp edge with humps along it. The underside, from the anus to the tail, is also a sharp edge. Use the No. 5/20 to pare the wood away either side of the center line around the dorsal fin and along the dorsal ridge, leaving a sharp edge at the top and blending the cut evenly out to the original profile width on the body. Do the same on the underside.

You will need to return to this area to carve the humps along the dorsal ridge when you have finished carving the detail of the tail.

25 (See **A**, **C** and **D**.) The sides of a whale's body feature two quite large, horizontal, muscle-like grooves along their length, from the area just behind the pectoral fins right back to the tail. Use the No. 7/20 to carve these grooves quite deeply, leaving the space in between them naturally bulging like a muscle.

26 (See **A**, **C** and **D**.) Blend these areas together with the No. 3/20.

27 (See **A**, **C** and **D**.) Sand over the entire area with 100-grit.

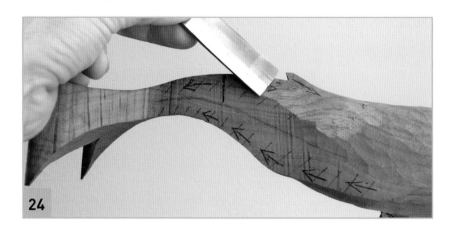

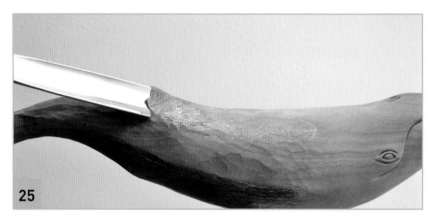

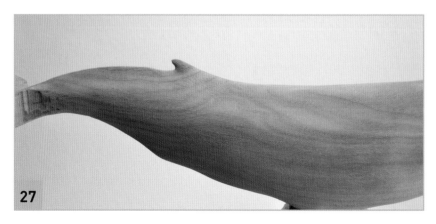

28a

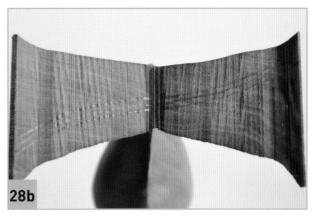

28b

29

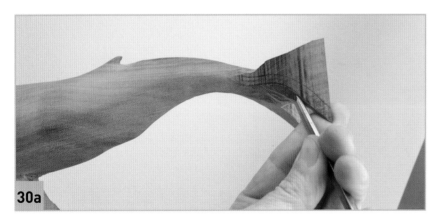

30a

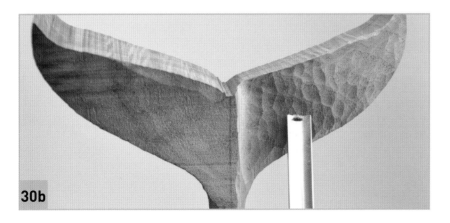

30b

Flukes

Carving the whale's flukes is a delicate operation and should be approached with patience and finesse – although they are probably not quite as fragile as they would appear due to the strength of the walnut wood and the direction of the grain. We also use the optical illusion of creating a very delicate sharp edge along the leading and rear edges of the flukes, but this tapers into the thicker body of them, meaning that they are, in fact, quite strong.

Study some real-life images of a whale's tail before you begin. Note how the tail emerges from the sides of the body (see **35b** on page 181), the areas of the dorsal ridge and underside merge into the tail (see **33** and **34** on page 180) and how the edges of the flukes are formed (see **35a** and **35b** on page 181).

28 (See **E** and **F**.) There is a little room for some artistic license here, as there is plenty of depth in the wood for you to create whatever angle you choose across the tail. You can follow the design shown here if

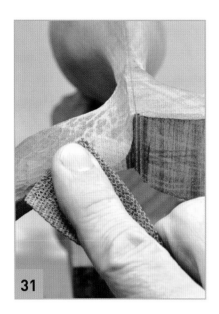

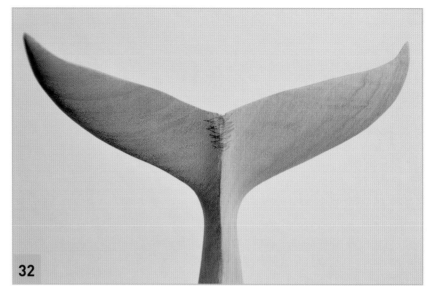

you wish or work with your own ideas – the technique will be the same. Draw the shape of the tail along the leading **28a** and rear edges **28b**, at approximately ¼in (6mm) thick and with a center line down through the middle.

29 (See **F**.) Use the knife to begin with and gently start to pare the wood back towards the line on the upper and lower sides of the tail.

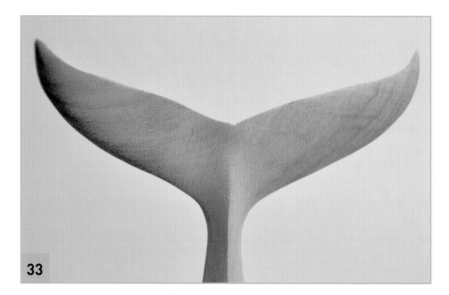

30 (See **C**.) As you work your way towards the line, the knife will become less effective and you will need to continue with the No. 7/6 **30a**. Use this to carve the depth of the tail evenly over the surface **30b**, down to the position of the lines at the leading and rear edges of the tail.

31 (See **A**, **B**, **C**, **D**, **E** and **F**.) Use a piece of 100-grit sandpaper to sharpen the edges of the tail down to the center lines. Repeat steps 29–31 on the opposite side of the tail.

32 (See **A**, **B**, **C**, **D**, **E** and **F**.) The dorsal ridge and underside of the body merge into the tail about halfway down its length; therefore you will need to carve the natural curvature of these upper and lower edges, blending them evenly into the tail at this point, and pare the wood back flush from this position to the back edge of the tail. Do this with the No. 7/6.

33 Your tail should now look like this.

34 (See **A** and **B**.) The edges of a whale's flukes are said to be as individual as a human's fingerprints, so you have plenty of flexibility in how you choose to deal with them. However, do study some images of real-life flukes before you start to help you understand this detail. Mark the separation points of the flukes onto the surface of your wood, making sure that they are in no way symmetrical on both sides. Use the knife to delicately cut them along the entire edge of the tail and then sand them into their natural shape using a piece of 240-grit sandpaper.

35a

35b

35 (See **A**, **C** and **D**.) With the sharp line of the dorsal ridge now merged into the tail, the detail of the little humps along the dorsal ridge can be finished.

Measure and mark on your wood ½in (13mm) positions from the rear of the dorsal fin along the dorsal ridge to the

tail. Use the No. 8/7 to cut in between these positions **35a**, then use the No. 7/6 to sharpen the dorsal ridge again into the No. 8 cuts. Finally, sand with 100-grit to blend all the depths naturally together and soften the detail. Your dorsal ridge, rear end of the body and flukes should now look like picture **35b**.

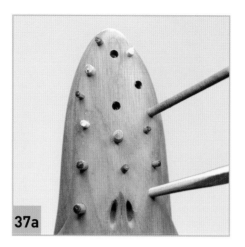

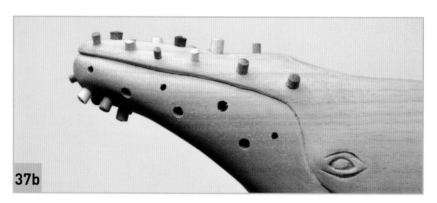

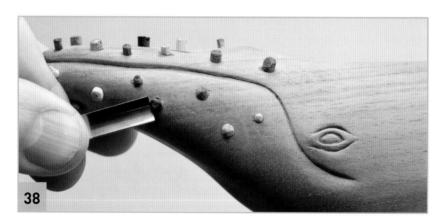

Tubercles

Have you ever wondered what the bumps are on a humpback whale's head? Well, they are called tubercles, and each one contains a sensory hair. In order to represent these tubercles in this project, it is more logical, realistic and, perhaps, creative, to add these to the whale, rather than carving them into the wood. Before you do this, it is best to sand the whale through the remaining grits so you don't need to fiddle around between the tubercles once they are inserted. Do this, using the hot-water technique (see page 63) in between each grit.

36 To prepare the wood for the tubercles, you must cut a selection of square $\frac{3}{32}$in and $\frac{1}{8}$in (2mm and 3mm) pieces in the various wood species that you intend to use. These can then simply be sanded with 100-grit on the four corners to produce round dowels ready for insertion into the drill holes, or, alternatively, if you have a

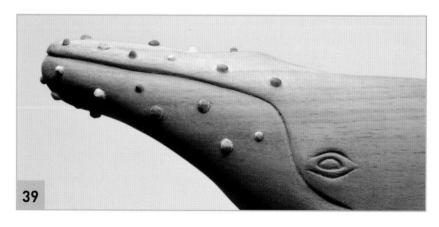

woodturning lathe you can turn them on that. (You can, of course, make some holes on a scrap of wood and practice the technique beforehand if you like.)

37 (See **Ⓐ**, **Ⓑ**, **Ⓒ**, **Ⓓ**, **Ⓔ** and **Ⓕ**.) Before you drill your holes, study some pictures of a humpback whale's head to see how the tubercles are formed around it. The majority appear to have them along the center line of the rostrum, the edge of the upper and lower sides of the mouth and around the chin plate, which also has many barnacles on it as well.

Mark where you intend to drill your ³⁄₃₂in and ⅛in (2mm and 3mm) holes. Make a mark on, or place a small strip of masking tape on, your drill bit approximately ³⁄₁₆in (5mm) from the cutting end. This will be a depth stop for you to work to. Drill all of the smaller holes first and then the larger ones down to the depth-stop position. Sand over all of the holes with 400-grit to clean up any flaky edges.

Working through each hole one at a time, push your chosen dowel stick into it **37a**. If it is a bit tight, simply sand it back a little more. When it fits tightly in, make a mark about ⅛in (3mm) proud of the surface. Take the dowel out of the hole, and cut it off at this position with a knife. Plug it back in and move onto the next one **37b**.

40a

When you have made them all, the next job is to glue them in place. Be very careful not to spill any adhesive on the head, as this could seal the grain and make the finish look rather patchy when it is finally oiled or waxed.

Remove each little dowel, one at a time. Place a spot of glue (instant glue, PVA, epoxy resin or whatever you prefer) in the hole. Push the dowel back into the hole. Hold another piece of dowel on top of it and give it a gentle tap with your mallet to seat it firmly in position. Repeat the procedure with all of the dowels and leave them to dry.

38 (See **Ⓐ**, **Ⓑ**, **Ⓒ**, **Ⓓ**, **Ⓔ** and **Ⓕ**.) Use the No. 7/6 to cut each dowel in a random, knobbly, roundish shape.

39 (See **Ⓐ**, **Ⓑ**, **Ⓒ**, **Ⓓ**, **Ⓔ** and **Ⓕ**.) Finally, sand them off with a piece of 400-grit to produce the finished tubercles.

40b

Ventral pleats

The ventral pleats are wrinkled skin that can expand massively when the whale is feeding. These run from the tip of the jaw back beyond the navel on the belly. Because the laminated block is underneath the whale's belly, you won't be able to carve the full length of the pleats until you cut the whale off the block. The grain of the wood is not lending itself to this detail here either because of the direction of the curvature of the body. So just do the best you can and worry about the rest later.

40 (See **Ⓑ**, **Ⓒ** and **Ⓓ**.) Use the ventral- and lateral-view scale drawings as a reference and draw the pleats in position, from the edge of the jaws across the surface of the belly **40a**. Use the knife to cut all of these slits, making an initial shallow cut to produce the tram line, followed by a deeper one **40b**. Make sure that you strop the knife ten times each side in between every cut.

41 (See **B**.) Use the No. 2/5, working from the belly forward to the chin, curving each pleat into the knife cut. Repeat steps 40 and 41 again if necessary to create the realistic effect.

42 (See **B**.) Sand the pleats with 100-grit to soften them and make them more naturalistic.

Pectoral fins

43 To enhance the life and movement in this project, the pectoral fins have been designed individually so that they project from the body at slightly different angles from one another. They will also be attached to the body at different angles to add to the realistic effect. If the fins were identical in angle and projection, the whale would look very stiff and unnatural. Whales' pectoral fins seem to come in many shapes and sizes, so do make your own design based on your own research if you wish to.

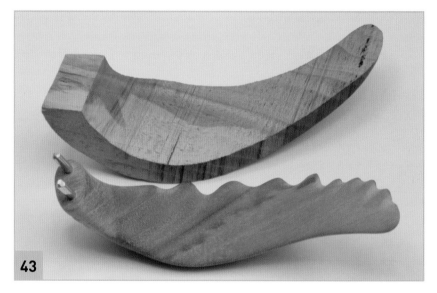

The wood that you use for your fins should obviously be of the same species as the body, and preferably from the same plank of wood so that the grain color is perfectly matched. The piece used for the example shown here had some lighter sapwood in the grain, which lent itself very nicely to the subject, as humpback whale fins are white underneath with patches of white on the top surface as well.

Use the templates provided to cut the two fin profiles out of your block of wood. Measure and draw center lines all of the way around the edges of the fins.

The pectoral fins need to be carved hand-held, which is not ideal but is perfectly safe as long as you follow these safety rules:

- Never carve in the direction of your fingers or hands.

- Make sure that your tools are razor sharp to eliminate any chance of them slipping.

- Hold the gouges in the same way as you would a pencil, at about 1in (25mm) away from the cutting edge (see **44** and **49** on the facing page and **50** and **52** on page 186).

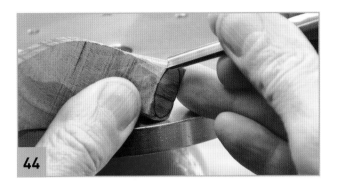

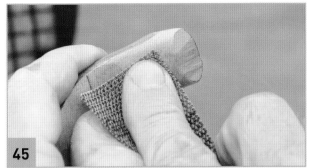

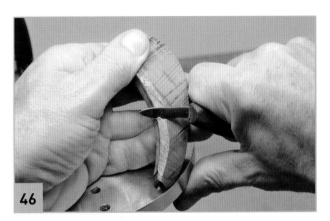

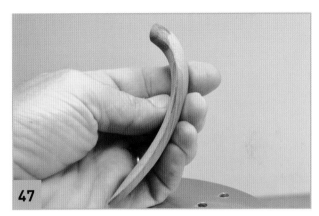

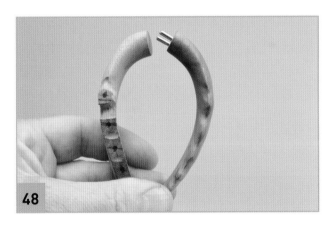

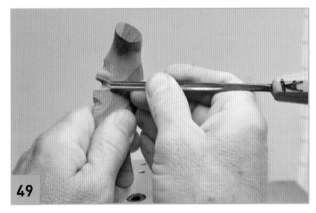

- Always try to have your ring finger (right hand) touching the wood to help give you good balance and control – better still, use your little finger as well if possible.

- Make very shallow cuts so that the tool cuts the wood easily and you are not straining your fingers with the pressure, thus avoiding the possibility of slipping.

44 Draw a ⅝in (17mm) ellipse on the edge of the fin where it will be attached to the whale. Use the No. 7/6 to pare the wood carefully back to this line.

45 Use a piece of 100-grit to naturally shape this area.

46 Use the knife to pare the rear edges of the fin down to the center line.

47 Use the 100-grit to blend the depths and sharpen the rear edge.

48 Use your template as a reference to help you mark the high position of the bumps along the leading edge of the fin.

49 Use a No. 8/4 to produce the deeper grooves in between the high bumps.

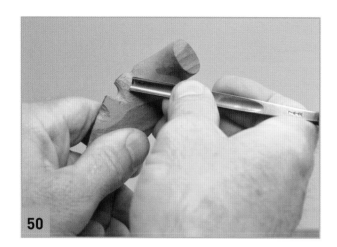

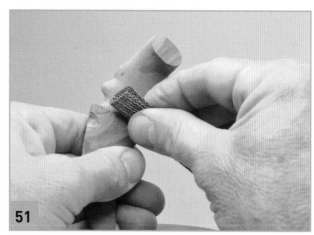

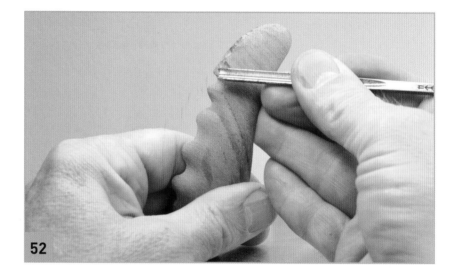

50 Use the No. 7/6 to pare this area back on both sides, making the leading bumpy edge thinner but not sharp like the rear edge.

51 Use a piece of 100-grit to finish the shaping of the leading edge, naturally curving the bumps and softening their appearance.

52 Repeat steps 49–51 along the leading edge until you reach the smaller bumps near the end of the fin. Now swap the No. 8/4 for a No. 11/3 to produce these smaller bumps to the end of this edge.

When you have finished carving the detail of the leading edge, sand the entire fin through the other grades of sandpaper (150, 240 and 400), using the hot-water technique in between each one (see page 63).

The fins are now complete and are ready to be attached to the whale's body.

53 To attach the fins to the body convincingly, you have to be extremely accurate both with the shape of the end of the fin that joins the body and the positioning of the pins that attach the fin and body together. The simplest and most effective way to achieve this is to pin the fin to the body first and then joint the fin into the body afterwards.

First, you need to make a separate template of the edge of each fin. Hold the fin on its edge on a piece of card and draw around the profile with a sharpened pencil. Cut this out carefully.

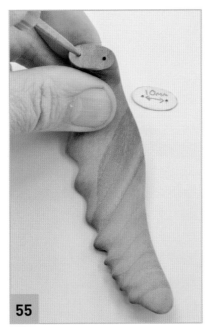

54 Mark two positions on the template ⅜in (10mm) apart at equal distances from the outer edges.

55 Hold the template in position on the edge of the fin and mark the two holes on the fin with a bradawl. Remove the template and use the bradawl again to make the holes slightly deeper so that the drill bit will not slip.

56 Measure the depth that you need to stop the drill holes at, to ensure that the bit doesn't come right through the fin. It should be approximately ⁵⁄₁₆in (8mm) on the left fin, and ¼in (6mm) on the right. Use a high-speed steel (HSS) drill bit the same size as your metal pin or wooden dowel – I used ³⁄₃₂in (2.4mm) metal pins. Make a mark or wrap a piece of masking tape around the drill bit at the depth at which you need to stop the hole, then slowly drill the hole, stopping frequently to make sure that the drill bit is going squarely into the fin, checking from the side and top views. Correct the angle if necessary and drill to the depth of your stop mark.

57 You now need to use the fin template again on the body of the whale in the precise position where you will be attaching the fin. Using your left and right lateral-view scale drawings for reference, measure the exact positioning of each fin on both sides of the body. Hold the template in position, carefully mark the drill holes and use the bradawl again to make small holes for the drill bit to seat into.

58 Drill the holes using the same technique as you used in step 56, to a depth of approximately ½in (13mm).

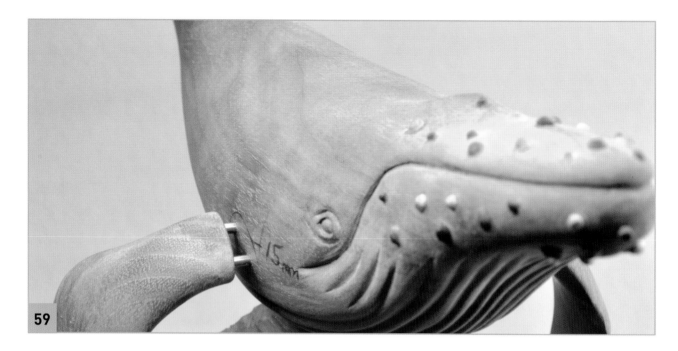

59 Calculate the depth of the drill holes, both into the fin and the body, and subtract approximately ⅛in (2–3mm). Cut your pins or dowels to this size and insert them into the fin. Plug the fin into the body. (If the pins/dowels do not line up correctly, check which pin/dowel is out of line, place the drill bit back into the hole and slightly move the drill to the misaligned side while it is in motion.) Push the fin up tight against the body and mark precisely around its edge with a sharpened pencil. Remove the fin again.

60 Use gouges of the same curvature as the fin's edge to cut precisely along the line. I used a No. 8/7 and the knife for mine.

61 Use the No. 2/5 to pare back the wood carefully in between the gouge/knife cuts. Repeat steps 60 and 61 until you reach a depth of approximately

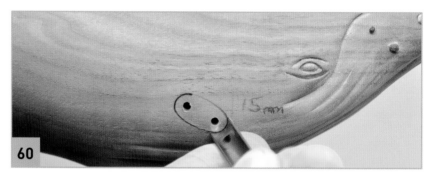

¹⁄₁₆in (1.5mm), or when the edge of the fin seats into the carved recess convincingly from all angles. Repeat steps 57 to 61 on both sides of the whale.

62 The final job to do before you cut your whale off its base is to add the slits on the body above the fins. You can also add two or three little ones across the connecting edge of the pectoral fins. These slits are

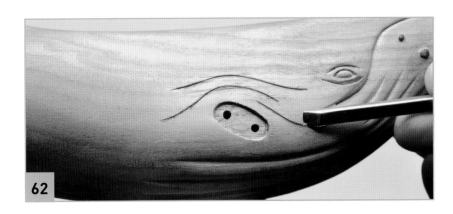

62

63

made using the same technique as you used for the ventral pleats (see pages 183–184). Use the right and left lateral-view drawings as a reference to help you draw the slits in position onto both sides of the body. Use the knife to cut along your lines and the No. 2/5 to pare the wood into the knife cuts. Sand through all the different grits to naturally soften these areas and bring them up to a fine finish.

63 Your carving should now look like this and can be cut off its base. Do this as near to the belly line as possible.

64 (See **B**.) You can now finish the ventral pleats on the whale's belly, either by carving hand-held or by securing the whale with a clamp or in a vise. If you choose the latter, great care must be taken with the tail, dorsal fin and clamping positions so as not to mark or break any of the details. Use your ventral-view scale drawing as a reference to draw the continuation of the lines of the ventral pleats and use the same techniques as in steps 40 to 42 to produce the pleats. Sand the pleats through all of the grits, using the hot-water technique in between each one and blending them softly together. Your whale is now complete.

64

65

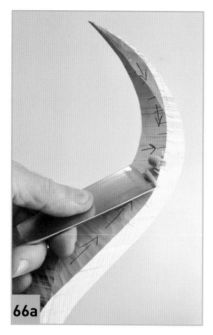

66a

66b

Sea mount

English cherry was chosen in this example for its strength and complementary color contrast to the whale. The dimensions are H 11¾ x W 6¼ x D 3½in (298 x 159 x 89mm).

I designed the movement in the whale so that it could be presented on a mount in any number of different artistic ways, and I would encourage you to design your own mount on which to present yours. But, if you would like to follow my simple design, then this is how to make it.

Before you start work on the Sea Mount, study the finished piece on page 167 to help you visually understand the detail that you will be producing.

65 Use the scale drawings provided to transfer the designs onto your wood and cut out both of the profiles.

66 The idea here is to enhance the movement of the whale by mounting it in a diving position and slightly listed over onto its left side. To produce this angle, mass is removed from the opposite edges on the front and rear sides of the wood, creating a gentle flowing angle from the base up through the 'sea'.

Use the No. 3/30, working along the right-hand edge of the front side, paring off approximately ⅜in (10mm) along this side, then gradually tapering it back out to a straight edge again at the lower outer curve of the design **66a**. Do the same on the rear side but work along the opposite edge, paring off about ⅜in (10mm) and tapering it back out to a straight edge again at the lower inner curve of the design **66b**.

67 Remove the bandsawn extension at the base with the No. 3/30 **67a** and **67b**.

68 The design can now be naturally angled around to flow from the base up into the curve to produce an effective, gently flowing contour. Do this with the No. 3/30. When you are sure that the mount is balanced correctly, sand it through all of the grits, using the hot-water technique in between each one.

69 The whale is secured to the mount using basically the same technique as the fins (see pages 187–188). The two pins/dowels should be placed centrally into the left and right ventral pleats, either side of the two middle ones and at the position where the body has the least curvature along its length, approximately 5½in (140mm) back from the tip of the nose. It is not so crucial to make a template here, but you must be absolutely accurate with your measurements between the drill holes.

67a

67b

68

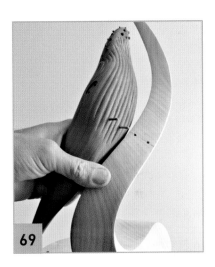

69

Measure, mark with the bradawl and drill your holes squarely into the whale first, to a depth of approximately ¾in (20mm). Transfer the measurements between the drill holes from the whale onto your mount at approximately 5in (128mm) down from the top. Measure the thickness of the area that you are about to drill and mark a stop position on your drill bit so that you don't drill right through it. Now drill both holes squarely and precisely in their correct positions and cut your pins or dowels to size. Insert them into the whale first then attach the whale to the mount.

For extra stability, the mount will also need to be mounted itself onto a base of your choice. This could be either wood, acrylic, glass, stone or whatever you wish to use. The finished sculpture on page 167 is mounted on a piece of 1³⁄₁₆in-thick (30mm) black granite measuring 5½ x 4½in

(140 x 115mm), which sits quietly underneath the mount and adds plenty of weight and stability to the structure. A piece of self-adhesive baize was stuck on the underside of the granite to cover the screw holes and protect any surfaces that it will be placed upon.

If you wish to fix the pectoral fins to the whale's body and the whale to its mount permanently, then epoxy resin is recommended to bond these pieces into position. However, the fins, whale and mount should all fit tightly enough together using the pins without the need for permanently gluing them. By doing this, it will be far easier to repolish the piece, as it can be deconstructed. Plus, if you ever need to transport the carving or pack it away then you can easily take it apart and package it safely in a box.

Finishing

The finish used for the whale and mount on page 167 was a thin application of boiled linseed oil, which darkened the wood and enhanced the natural beauty of the grain. It was left for a week to dry before a dark wax polish was applied. This added a wonderful sheen to the surface and gave depth to the grain. You can use the same finish or experiment with your own ideas.

Suppliers

Sawmill, lumber tools and machinery
Yandle and Son Ltd
+44 (0)1953 822 207
www.yandles.co.uk

Lumber
John Boddy Timber Ltd
+44 (0)1423 322 370
www.john-boddy-timber.ltd.uk

Lincolnshire Woodcraft Supplies
+44 (0)1780 757 825
www.lincolnshirewoodcraft.co.uk

Lumber and other materials
S.L. Hardwoods Ltd
+ 44 (0)20 8683 0292
www.slhardwoods.co.uk

Hydra clamp work positioners
WDS Component Parts Ltd
+ 44 (0)113 290 9852
www.wdsltd.co.uk

Sculptor's tools, materials and studio equipment
Alec Tiranti Ltd
+ 44 (0)845 123 2100
www.tiranti.co.uk

Tools, equipment and materials
Axminster Tool Centre
+ 44 (0)800 371 822
www.axminster.co.uk

Craft Supplies Ltd
+ 44 (0)1433 622 550
www.craft-supplies.co.uk

Highland Woodworking
+1 404 872 4466
www.highlandwoodworking.com

Tilgear
+ 44 (0)845 099 0220
www.tilgear.info

Treeline
+1 800 598 2743
www.treelineusa.com

Woodcraft
+1 800 225 1153
www.woodcraft.com

Abrasives, tools and materials
CSM Abrasives Plus
+ 44 (0)1636 688 888
www.abrasivesplus.com

Tool manufacturers
Festool
Worldwide: www.festool.com
UK: www.festool.co.uk
USA: www.festoolusa.com
Germany: www.festool.de

Henry Taylor Tools Ltd
+ 44 (0)114 234 0282 / 234 0321
www.henrytaylortools.co.uk

Hermes Abrasives Ltd
+ 44 (0)1206 75 44 00
www.hermes-abrasives.co.uk

Kirschen
Worldwide: www.kirschen.de
Australia: www.kirschen.com.au

KWH Mirka
Finland
+ 358 (0)20 760 2111
www.mirka.com

Pfeil
(Schaller is also made by Pfeil)
Switzerland
+ 41 (0)62 922 45 65
www.pfeiltools.com

Stubai
Austria
+ 43 5225 6960-0
www.stubai.com

Bibliography

Barcsay, J., **Anatomy for the Artist**
Metro Books, 2001

Butz, R., **How to Sharpen Carving Tools**
Stackpole Books, 1997

Drudi, E., **Figure Drawing for Fashion Design**
Pepin Pr, 2010

Goldfinger, E., **Human Anatomy for Artists,
The Elements of Form**
OUP USA, 1992

Hasluck, P. N., **Manual of Traditional Wood Carving**
Dover Publications, 1977

Hogarth, B., **Drawing the Human Head**
Watson-Guptill Publications, 1989

Hogarth, B., **Dynamic Anatomy**
Watson-Guptill Publications, 1990

Hogarth, B., **Dynamic Light and Shade**
Watson-Guptill Publications, 1991

Hogarth, B., **Dynamic Wrinkles and Drapery**
Watson-Guptill Publications, 1995

Lucchesi, B., **Modeling the Figure in Clay**
Watson-Guptill Publications, 1996

Lucchesi, B., **Modeling the Head in Clay**
Watson-Guptill Publications, 1991

Norbury, I., **Carving Classical Female Faces
in Wood**
Fox Chapel Publishing, 2004

Norbury, I., **Carving Classical Female Figures
in Wood**
Stobart Davies Limited, 2004

Norbury, I., **Fundamentals of Figure Carving**
Linden Publishing, 1993

Pipes, A., **Foundations of Art and Design**
Laurence King, 2008

Pye, C., **Tools, Materials and Equipment Volume 1**
Guild of Master Craftsman Publications Ltd, 2002

Pye, C., **Tools, Materials and Equipment Volume 2**
Guild of Master Craftsman Publications Ltd, 2002

Simblet, S., **Anatomy for the Artist**
Dorling Kindersley Publishing, 2001

**Woodcarving Illustrated, Best of Wood Carving
Illustrated, Woodcarver's Guide to Sharpening
Tools and Setting Up Shop**
Fox Chapel Publishing, 2010

About the Author

Andrew Thomas has been a professional sculptor since 1993 and rapidly gained international recognition for his three-dimensional art, which has won him over 20 awards during his career, including three international gold medals. His work has also garnered him high acclaim in the UK's most prestigious exhibitions and academies, including the Royal West of England Academy, the Royal British Society of Artists, Mall Galleries London, Olympia London and Henley Festival, and is currently hosted by many fine-art galleries nationwide.

By experimentation with form over many years, Andrew has progressively developed his understanding of three-dimensional sculpture, naturally evolving his individual style of work to produce an extensive and diverse range of harmonious designs, in a number of series, all embodying the essence of their subject. His work is created in the beautiful, tactile medium of wood and then cast into bronze limited editions, which are recognized for their elegant fusion of plane and contour, full of dynamic energy, graceful movement and emotional resonance, sensitively breathing life into the spaces that they occupy.

This depth of experience and perception of three-dimensional form has enabled him to architect a structured, and highly successful method of tuition, which logically disentangles its complexities and illuminates the fundamental techniques and creative skills that are essential in order to successfully produce both realistic and artistic forms. Andrew is a qualified tutor with almost two decades of teaching experience, both in further education and privately from his studio where he delivers tuition sessions that accommodate the level of ability and specific interests of each individual student who wishes to learn this challenging and fascinating subject.

For more information about Andrew, his work and tuition visit his website: www.3dsculptor.com.

Acknowledgments

Working with three-dimensional form has been an extraordinary and illuminating journey throughout my life, and I feel very blessed to have had the good fortune to be able to explore its creative lengths and breadths. This would not have been possible without the unwavering, selfless support, patience, belief, encouragement and love from my wife, Christine Thomas, to whom I owe so very much – thank you. I must also thank the other members of my family: Jacob Luke, Myrna, Army, Simon, Katy, John, Ethal, Mike, Jeanne, David and Debbie for their endless support and encouragement over a lifetime of work.

My students have all individually contributed enormously to the experience that I have gathered over the years, so I would like to mention some of them to show my appreciation: Helen Burns, Phil Carter, Syd Coule, John Fossey, Ray Harris, Wendy and Tony Tabb, David Whiddett, Robbie Way, Tony Roots, Pauline Gover, Tom McClellan, Ellis Hobbs, Linda Hume, Kim Sneddon and Jason Watkins.

I would like to thank Jamie Hart for supplying an image of his work, 'External Oblique,' for me to use in the Wood chapter and Wendy Tab (Indian), John Fossey (Horse's Head), Ray Harris (Tudor Rose) and Phil Carter (Arthes) for allowing me to use images of their work in the chapters on Tools and Effective Sanding. Thanks also to Christine Zulauf from Pfeil Tools for providing the Swiss numbering-system chart.

I would like to thank Mark Baker, the Group Editor of GMC's woodworking magazines, for the excellent collaboration we have shared over many years, for his forward thinking and vision and for his steadfast trust and belief in the work that I have produced for his publications. Thanks also to Gerrie Purcell from GMC Publications and a very special thanks to Dominique Page and Simon Smith who have assisted me throughout the production of this book.

Picture credits

Photos and illustrations by Andrew Thomas except for the following:
Christine Thomas: pages 17, 31 (top), 194
Lanarkshire Hardwoods (www.lanarkshirehardwoods.co.uk): pictures 13 and 18 on page 47
Pfeil: 24–25
Simon Rodway: pages 42, 43 (top left, middle left)

All carvings by Andrew Thomas except for the following:
'Horse' by John Fossey: page 15 (top)
'Tudor Rose' by Ray Harris: page 21 (bottom)
'Indian' by Wendy Tabb: pages 62 (top), 64 (top right) and 65 (middle right)
'Arthes' – Welsh name for 'She-Bear' – by Phil Carter: page 65 (middle left)

Index

Titles of projects are indicated by **bold** print.

To place an order or to request a catalog, contact:

The Taunton Press, Inc.

63 S. Main Street, PO Box 5506, Newtown, CT 06470-5506

Tel (800) 888-8286

www.taunton.com